MW00949509

WAITING FOR THE TRAIN

Biblical Food for Growing Before Going

S. Tory Teller

WestBow Press books may be ordered through booksellers or by contacting:

WestBow Press
A Division of Thomas Nelson & Zondervan
1663 Liberty Drive
Bloomington, IN 47403
www.westbowpress.com
844-714-3454

ISBN: 978-1-6642-3222-8 (sc)
ISBN: 978-1-6642-3223-5 (hc)
ISBN: 978-1-6642-3221-1 (e)

Library of Congress Control Number: 2021908169

Print information available on the last page.

WestBow Press rev. date: 05/21/2021

COMMENTS ABOUT WAITING FOR THE TRAIN

We all know that stories are often more powerful than preaching, especially when the voice of the storyteller is trusted and authentic. They fly under the radar and rarely cause people to set up their defenses. However, we also know that there is a place for preaching that calls us to take seriously the word of God. What happens when you combine the straightforwardness of preaching with the warmth of personal stories? That is exactly what the author has done with this collection of his personal journal entries now made available to all of us.

Fred Smith, founder of The Gathering

****

There are many great devotionals, but I've never read any like Waiting for the Train. *With each reading you will walk through a section of Scripture and learn, through the enjoyable dialogue, both the word of God and how it applies to every day of your life. Soon you will feel as though you are part of the friendship and conversation that these two characters share. I have encouraged our entire Men's Ministry to read the online version, and I believe you will enjoy what you have in your hands!*

Troy Dewey, Men's Pastor, Maranatha Chapel, San Diego, California

****

In this day of increasingly superficial Christian living, the author has delivered a series of the most insightful, spiritually penetrating, and powerful messages I've seen God use in my life and others to draw us to Himself. I fully recommend this book as you discover the wisdom that overflows from a man who has been walking with Jesus deeply for many years.

Dr. Ron Jensen, author, speaker and chairman of High Ground

****

In a world and time with so much division, this book is a daily breath of fresh air. S. Tory Teller sets forth solid Biblical truth in a very relaxed and engaging way. A great devotional for younger believers to get grounded in Biblical truth, as well as for more mature believers to learn how to share their view in a conversational, engaging way. I highly recommend this book for all who desire to walk in a manner worthy of Jesus!

Tiger Dawson, CEO & co-founder, Edify
****

Here is a very non-threatening way to share the truth in love, addressing serious questions that everyone deals with in their spiritual journey. Each exchange is brief, targeted, and refreshing to read. The author has bridged the gap between those wanting to grow as maturing Christians and those just seeking to understand what it means to be a Christian. It is ideal as a daily devotional to nurture our existing walk with God or as an evangelistic tool to share with someone who doesn't know God. It's rare when one book can do both, and this book does it beautifully.

Gil Mertz, pastor and author of *Forgive Your Way to Freedom*
****

The world is full of believers who struggle to grow spiritually and build in the daily practices that lead to maturity in Christ. The author has created a unique and creative story-based devotional series to help us do just that. Waiting for the Train *is an intriguing way to help anyone follow Jesus, whether their journey is just starting or whether they've been at it for decades.*

Kevin Palau, president of Luis Palau Association
****

I have found this very unique devotional an extremely useful tool in leading followers of Jesus to a more mature faith, both for new and not-so-new believers. The fact that each reading deals with one main point makes it very digestible to anyone wrestling with the essence of a closer walk with God. The conversations are suitable to all ages and are thoughtful reminders of truth for all of us. The closing prayer is "icing on the cake!"

Terry Parker, Esq., co-founder National Christian Foundation

****

Waiting for the Train *is your daily ticket for keeping your spiritual growth "on the rails!" Born out of his desire to learn what it means to be a disciple of Jesus Christ, the author has journaled prayers and devotions for 20+ years in his daily and personal study of God's word. The book you hold in your hands is the author's description of what a disciple looks like, one quality at a time. And the best part is, it's a fascinating story that will keep you reading!*

Paul Fleischmann, President Emeritus National Network of Youth Ministries

FOREWORD

Having spent my life bringing people to the truth of the gospel, as well as bringing that truth to them, I have always appreciated that Jesus was a great storyteller. His stories or parables help us understand the truth of what He said.

I think there is a place in today's world for stories that present what Jesus said in a different way, a way that resonates in truth without preaching and without overreaching. I think that is what this book presents.

Although the author of *Waiting for the Train* writes under a pseudonym and is not identified, I have known him for many years, and I appreciate how he has responded to God's leading in making these stories available to all who seek to grow in their faith walk.

Some of the stories in *Waiting for the Train* are biographical, some are memoir, and some are pure creative writing. Which is which does not matter. What does matter is the Biblical truth that is presented in a practical way.

"Make disciples" is what Jesus said to do when He gave His disciples the Great Commission. While the basic steps of discipleship are the same for everyone, how those steps are taken may differ for each person seeking to move toward spiritual maturity. I think *Waiting for the Train* provides insight for strengthening your faith, whether as a new believer or as one who, for whatever reason, has not moved towards greater faith. It does so in a unique way of a conversation between a mentor and one being mentored.

As the mentor, Stan, and the one telling the stories sit having breakfast, you can overhear their conversation. As you listen to the stories being told, as you "join in the conversation," I think you will be helped along the path towards greater spiritual maturity with deeper faith. That is my prayer for you. Enjoy what you have in your hands. Let it make a difference in how you grow before you go, while you wait for the train!

Josh McDowell

INTRODUCTION

This book consists of a selection of readings that appeared originally, in different form, on the website www.waiting4thetrain.com. The postings on that site are based on the author's twenty-plus years of daily journaling which, in essence, is a written conversation with God. That conversation flows from reading and studying Scripture, praying, and listening to the Holy Spirit. Each chapter in this book is intended to help you in the process of maturing as a Christian, whether you are a new believer or one who wants to continue on the path of growth in Christ. If you are not yet a believer, there's still time before the train leaves. Welcome!

The storyline begins when the narrator, S. Tory Teller, has just become a Christian but does not know what to do next. Proceeding to find out, he is led to a man named Stan, who becomes his mentor, discipling him in his faith as they meet regularly for conversation over breakfast.

Each conversation is followed by scriptures that connect to that day's theme. Then there is a prayer that leads to deeper understanding. Finally, there are "Think on This" points intended to stimulate further thought and discussion with others who are also "waiting for the train." I encourage you to write your thoughts. Journaling has made a significant difference in my faith walk, and it may in yours as well.

CONTENTS

DAY 1

Waiting for the Train: Assurance of Salvation and What it Means for This Life

I approached the train station, surprised no one was there.

As I stood on the platform looking from one direction to the other, the station master approached. "Need any help?" he asked.

"Can you tell me when the next train is due to arrive?" I said.

"Depends on where you're headed'" he replied.

"This is what I have." I showed him my ticket. "I think it's good for a one-way trip to glory."

"Where did you get this?" the station master asked, and then added, "Do you know what it means?"

"I got it from a fellow on a corner downtown; he was talking about glory and giving out tickets."

"I know him," the station master replied. "He's a good one! How much did you pay?"

"Nothing," I said, "the fellow promised it was free."

"Good," said the station master. "That's the only way it works. Someone else paid the full price, so you only need to accept it. You couldn't buy this kind of ticket even if you tried. You'd be surprised how many people show up here with a worthless ticket. There's a lot of shock and sadness when I tell them they were sold something that's no good. But that's another story for another day."

Then he asked me, "What about you? Did you think you could get on any train you prefer, at any time?"

"Well, I'm not sure," I replied, "but I'm real tired of where I am and anxious to leave. The ticket fellow made glory sound so good, I want to get there as soon as I can."

The station master shook his head. "That's not how the ticket works. Do you see any people just standing around waiting for a train?"

"No," I said. "That's what surprised me about this station. Can you tell me more about the train to glory? Is the ticket any good? Do I need a reservation?"

The station master smiled. "Yes, the ticket is good, and no, you don't need a reservation. When the train arrives, there will be a seat for you."

"Great!" I replied. "So when's the next train going to arrive?"

"I don't know," he said.

"You don't know? That's a funny way to run a railroad."

"It's not up to you and it's not up to me," was his solemn response.

"But what am I supposed to do? Just sit around and wait?"

"No," said the station master, "you are to give away tickets."

Now I was exasperated. "I don't have any tickets to give away," I whined, "and there's no one here anyway!"

The station master answered with great patience. "The people who come to this platform already have a valid ticket. Your duty is to leave here and find people who lack tickets. And don't worry," he added, "you will be given tickets to give away when the time is right."

"But what do I tell people? I don't understand the tickets myself."

"You will be instructed," was all he said.

"But if I leave here, give away tickets, and tell people what the ticket means, I might miss the train when it comes."

"Won't happen" was his quick reply. "The train will only come when you are on the platform, and you will know when it's time to come back to catch the train."

Still confused, I asked, "Can't I just stay here until the train comes?"

The station master laughed. "You might get awfully tired of standing! Do you see anything to sit on? I want you to note especially there are no rocking chairs and none of those fancy chairs that recline. This platform is intended for one purpose only, and that is to leave for glory."

I was silent, so he continued. "If you did choose to stand around waiting, the train would eventually arrive for you. But that would be pure folly and a waste of your life. So many people not only don't have a ticket, they don't even know there's a train. And a whole world of ticket holders don't know the true meaning of what they have been given."

Then, in a voice of real authority, the station master said, "Go and tell people about the train and where it goes. Give out tickets as opportunity arises and explain what they mean. When it is time for you to return to this platform, you will have done what was expected of you."

With his gentle smile, he added, "I will be waiting here to open the train door for you." Then, overcoming all my hesitation, he repeated the command: "Go."

And that is what I am seeking to do.

Bible verses to consider:

For God so loved the world, that He gave His only begotten Son, that whoever believes in Him should not perish, but have eternal life. John 3:16.

And this is eternal life, that they may know Thee, the only true God, and Jesus Christ whom Thou hast sent. John 17:3.

Just as the body without the spirit is dead, so also faith without works is dead. James 2:26.

Work out your salvation with fear and trembling; for it is God who is at work in you, both to will and to work for His good pleasure. Philippians 2:12-13.

Prayer: Thank you, Father, for your provision of salvation through the finished work of Jesus Christ on the cross. Thank you that I know where I am going when it is time for me to step into eternity. It is clear that you have work for me to do before then. I ask you to lead me and help me according to your will. Thank you that I can bring these prayers before you in the name of Jesus. Amen.

Think on this: What does the "ticket to glory" look like? What does it mean that it cannot be bought? Do you have your ticket? If no, do you know what it takes to get one? If yes, do you know what you are to be doing while you wait for the train? Are you stuck on the platform, or have you left the station to give out tickets and explain what they mean? If so, what does that look like? If you aren't doing it, but want to, do you know how?

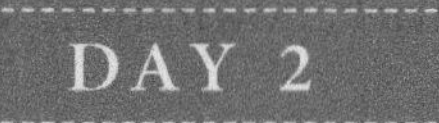

DAY 2

The First Steps

As I walked away from the train station, I had the recurring urge to look back. Each time I did, the station master was waving to me as if to say, "Be on your way." I eventually stopped looking back.

I walked towards the city park a few blocks away. I passed several people and wondered if I should stop and tell them about the tickets to glory. I had no idea what I would say, so I decided against it.

At the park I saw a man sitting alone on a bench. "Mind if I join you?" I asked.

In a gruff voice, he responded, "It's not my bench. Besides, this is a free country."

I sat down reluctantly. Several times I tried to open a conversation, hoping we could get on the subject of the train and tickets. But he was not much of a talker, and I was very nervous and unsure of myself.

The man eventually got up and walked away. I hadn't said anything that might affect his life and eternal destination. I felt disappointed in myself. Should I just go back to the station and wait for the train? "I better not," I thought to myself. "It might disappoint the station master."

I wandered across the park feeling pretty dejected. I saw a small crowd gathered around someone. As I got closer, I saw that it was none other than the man who had given me my ticket. As he spoke, more and more people asked him for a ticket.

"Oh, I wish I could be like that man" was the thought running through my head. When the crowd had dispersed and I was left alone with him, he asked, "Do you want a ticket?"

"You gave me one a while back, downtown," I responded.

"Sorry," he replied. "I give away so many that I can't always remember everyone. What are you doing in the park?" he asked.

I told him about going to the train station and talking with the station master. Then I described my experience with the man on the bench and how I felt like a failure.

"There are no failures among those who have tickets," was his quick response. "Some may feel like failures because they aren't comfortable meeting people and explaining the tickets. But there are lots of other things they can do."

"Like what?" I asked eagerly.

"In the first place," he said, "People who give out tickets need lots of support. Other ticket holders can help in many ways. And as the station master told you, there is a great need for people to help others understand what the ticket means. That is a vital role for all ticket holders."

"Bottom line is this: if you are open to seeing, God will show you all sorts of things you can do while waiting for the train."

My curiosity was growing. "Can you explain more about this?" I asked.

"Sure," he said. "Getting the ticket to glory is just the beginning. Unfortunately, too many ticket holders don't do anything but clutch their own ticket. They hold it real tight, thinking that is all they need. It is all they need to get to glory, but they fail to recognize that they are called to be something they have never been and do things they have never done, before they get on the train."

"I think I'm beginning to understand," I said. "But who helps the ticket holders understand?"

"Other ticket holders who are doing what God wants to do in and through them," he replied.

"You don't know how happy this makes me," I said with a very large smile. "Maybe that's what I'm supposed to do!"

"Could be, and probably is," the ticket man responded. Then he patted me on the back and added, "In fact, I'm sure it is!"

Bible verses to consider:
He gave some as apostles, and some as prophets, and some as evangelists, and some as pastors and teachers, for the equipping of the saints for the work of service, to the building up of the body of Christ. Ephesians 4:11-12

Prayer: Thank you, Father, for your free and gracious gift of salvation through the life, death, and resurrection of Jesus Christ. Thank you I know where I am going when I board the train. Thank you, too, for the life you have given me to live while I wait for the train. As you know, I am at times uncertain what you intend for that life to be. I need your help in knowing how to follow your lead as you take me to where you want me to be. Thank you I can and do bring these prayers before you in the name of Jesus. Amen.

Think on this: We are all called to be and do what God has for us. We are to help others be who God intends them to be. It is a matter of being available to God. Are you as available as you want? If no, what more would you like to be doing? Do you know how?

DAY 3

Seeking and Finding Help

It was getting close to lunch time and I was hungry. I asked the ticket man if he would like to get a bite to eat. He said he knew a great little spot just around the corner called "Twelve Baskets."

"That's an unusual name," I said.

"It refers to the baskets of bread left over after Jesus fed a crowd of people long ago," he said.

"It's the place of choice for lots of ticket holders."

"Lead the way," I said.

As we entered the cafe, the ticket man nodded his greeting to people he obviously recognized, but as we were seated, he seemed to be looking for one particular person.

"Are you supposed to meet someone here?" I asked with a little disappointment.

"No," he responded, "but I was hoping he would be here so I could introduce you."

"Who?" I asked.

"A man I think can help you with some of the questions you have about your ticket."

We ordered lunch and engaged in some small talk. I had so many questions for him, but I just didn't know where to start.

Halfway through our meal, the ticket man looked up and said, "There he is—the man I want you to meet."

The ticket man waved at him, and he came over to the table. The ticket man explained that I was a new ticket holder with lots of questions.

"Be glad to help in any way I can," said the gentleman. "Stop by my table when you are done, and we can talk."

"Thank you very much," I replied."

I finished lunch with the ticket man, who said, "Sorry to eat and run, but I need to get back to the park."

"And I need to get over and talk with your friend," I said. "Thank you for spending so much time with me."

"My pleasure," he responded.

I looked around to see where the gentleman was seated. He motioned me over. I headed in his direction, not knowing I was about to begin an amazing journey.

I sat down, stuck out my hand, and said, "I'm sorry, but I didn't catch your name when we were introduced."

"You can call me Stan," he responded. "How do you happen to be here today?"

I told him about getting my ticket and going to the train station, then to the park. "All that's happening to me is new and foreign," I continued. "I don't really know what's going on."

He nodded knowingly, with a kind smile. "When I first got my ticket, I had no idea what it meant," he said. "I didn't go to the train station as you did; I simply didn't know what to do or where to go."

"Did you ever find out?"

"Yes," he said. "Some very kind ticket holders, who had been down the same road, took time out of their busy lives to help me. They were so helpful that I decided to spend my life doing the same."

Then, more solemnly, he asked, "Are you interested in finding out what this ticket is all about?"

"Absolutely," I replied. And so it began.

Bible verses to consider:
Iron sharpens iron, so one man sharpens another. Proverbs 27:17.

So then, my beloved, just as you have always obeyed, not as in my presence only, but now much more in my absence, work out your salvation with fear and trembling; for it is God who is at work in you, both to will and to work for His good pleasure. Philippians 2:12-13.

Prayer: Thank you, Father, for new beginnings. Thank you for your provision of life eternally with you when it's time. And thank you for your provision of people to help others understand what you have for them while they wait to join you in eternity. I want to know, receive, and embrace all you have for me. Please help me follow every step of your lead, as you show me those steps through all you bring into my life. Thank you I can and do bring these prayers before you in the name of Jesus. Amen.

Think on this: Having a spiritual mentor is a great step in knowing how to proceed down the path from conversion towards spiritual maturity. Do you have such a mentor? Would you like one? Why or why not? What are the ways to find one?

DAY 4

Being Serious About Growing Before Going

As I sat across from Stan, he said, "If it's okay with you, I'd like to talk about some fundamentals so you know what you might be getting into."

"What do you mean?" I asked.

"I spend a lot of my time helping different people seek maturity in their faith walk. Obviously, I only have the time God has allotted for me until I get on the train. And I take seriously what I think God has for me to do: help others understand where they are and where they can be in this life, this side of eternity, in their relationship with God. I give a lot of prayerful thought to how I might be used by God to help others. I think God has made it clear that I am to focus on those who are serious."

"So," I responded, "you want me to make sure I am serious before I make any sort of commitment. Is that what you're saying?"

"Exactly," Stan replied. "So please give it real thought, and don't just jump in."

"I will," I said. "Can we get together again, after I have a chance to think about this? It's all very new to me, and I want to head in the right direction."

"Of course," Stan responded. "Would later this afternoon be too soon?"

"I think that would work," I responded. "What time can we meet?"

"How about four o'clock? I would love to buy you a scone and a cup of coffee."

"Fabulous!" I responded. "I'll be here. Love scones."

"Great," he said. "We can discuss getting together on a regular basis."

"Thanks, Stan," I replied. "See you at four."

Bible verses to consider:
And the Spirit and the bride say "Come." . . . And let the one who is thirsty come; let the one who wishes take the water of life without cost. Revelation 22:17.

Draw near to God and He will draw near to you. James 4:8.

Prayer: Thank you, Father, for what you want to do in and through me. Thank you, too, for the people you bring into my life who are willing to share their knowledge of you. I want to know you as deeply as is humanly possible on this side of eternity. Please help me be serious about a deeper faith walk with you. I confess that too many times, my pursuit of knowing you has been hit and miss, mostly miss. Please forgive me. And please help me follow every step of your lead into a deeper relationship with you. Thank you for the people you bring into my life to help me to know you. And thank you that I can and do bring these prayers before you in the name of Jesus. Amen.

Think on this: Are you serious about your relationship with God? Do you want to pursue it as deeply as possible? Why or why not? What would it take for you to pursue a deeper relationship with God? How can you find out what God wants? The first place to begin is in prayer. God will graciously show you what is on His heart!

DAY 5

A Walk to the Truth

I was back at Twelve Baskets just before four o'clock. Stan arrived on time, and the waiter came to take our order. Stan introduced us. "This is Ricky," he said.

After Ricky served us coffee and blueberry scones, I didn't exactly know how to start the conversation. So I asked Stan, "Can you tell me how you got to where you are, in your relationship with God?"

"Be glad to," Stan replied. "It was a long walk for me to come to the truth. I don't want to bore you with too much detail, but if we decide to get together regularly, we can spend time talking about my journey, if it is helpful to you."

"Whatever you want," I replied.

"I didn't become a Christian and get my ticket to glory until I was well into adulthood. That was despite attending church most of my life. Attending, but not paying much attention."

"Something must have changed at some point. What was it?" I asked.

"God worked through His people," Stan said. "People who were obedient in bringing me to the truth, or rather, bringing the truth to me. But even with those people, the ones who invited me to church, the ones who presented the message of the truth, the ones who led Bible studies I was involved in, it still took me a long time, probably way too long, to accept the truth. However," he added, "to my eternal gratitude, one day I finally came to realize that sin separates a person from God. That's where I was and there was only one solution."

"What solution?" I asked.

"The cross of Christ," Stan replied. "Jesus went to the cross to pay the price to save me."

"Save you from what?" I asked.

"Eternal separation from God," Stan said. "Big subject. One we can talk about more if we get together. But, for the moment, the truth is that my sin separated me from God, I could do nothing about it on my own other than accept the free gift of salvation, and that's what I did."

"So," I replied, "end of story?"

"Yes and no," Stan said. "The end of being separated from God for eternity, but the beginning of being transformed into who and what God intends for me before then."

"What does 'being transformed' mean?" I asked.

"Another big subject," Stan said, "one to be tackled a little at a time. But to jump to the bottom line, transformation involves being changed from who and what I was into who and what God intends for me."

"And how does that happen?" I asked.

"Through the Holy Spirit, who is called the Helper," Stan responded. "Upon my acceptance of God's provision of eternal salvation, He sent the Holy Spirit, who is also called the Spirit of Truth, to lead, guide, counsel, and help me in being and in doing all that God intends for me. The Holy Spirit leads the transformation. The question is always whether I will follow. We can talk a lot about that as well."

Having heard what Stan had said, it was clear to me that I wanted to hear more. I said, "Stan, I would like to get on your calendar to spend some regular time with you."

"Good," he replied, "but I want to make sure you understand a couple of things. First, you having the relationship with God that He wants is up to you, not me. Secondly, I can help, but I can't make it happen. To repeat, it's up to you." Then he added, "How about starting next Wednesday morning? Eight o'clock. Here."

"Thank you. I'll be here," I replied. "Is there anything I should do to get ready for our meeting?"

"I suggest you spend time asking God what He has in mind. Ask and be sure to listen to what He says about what He wants you to be and do until it's time to go to the station and board the train."

With that we parted, and I looked forward to Wednesday.

Bible verses to consider:
I am the way, and the truth, and the life; no one comes to the Father, but through Me. John 14:6.

And I will ask the Father, and He will give you another Helper, that He may be with you forever; that is the Spirit of truth, whom the world cannot receive, because it does not behold Him or know Him, but you know Him because He abides with you, and will be in you. John 14:16-17.

Receive the Holy Spirit. John 20:22.

Prayer: Thank you, Father, for your guidance. Thank you for the people you bring into my life who can help me pursue spiritual maturity. I confess that too often I do not pursue what you intend because I want to do what I want to do apart from you. Please forgive me. Help me follow every step of your lead so I move on the path from conversion towards transformation, exactly as you intend. Father, open me to see, understand, receive, and embrace all you have for me as long as you keep me on this side of eternity. Thank you I can and do bring these prayers before you in the name of Jesus. Amen.

Think on this: Having a spiritual mentor is essential for growing before going. Having someone you can relate to is vital. Do you have such a mentor? If not, how might you go about finding one? Your pastor is a good place to start. What would it look like for you to be a spiritual mentor, helping others on the path toward spiritual maturity? Is that something you would like to do? Why or why not?

DAY 6

Spiritually Mature or Maturing Spiritually?

As I walked out of the cafe, I experienced the joy of anticipation. I had the sense that something significant was about to happen in my life. I purposefully avoided going by the train station.

During the week, I did something that was pretty new to me: I prayed. I didn't really know how, so I spent a lot of time just listening, something I had never done. I was definitely sensing I was starting a new journey, an adventure with God.

I felt peaceful in a way I could not understand. Hard to even describe.

Along with the peace was an excitement. Tuesday night came, but sleep did not. I was eager to talk with Stan about what I was feeling, to see if he could make sense of it for me. I prayed and asked God to give me sleep. The next thing I knew the sun was coming up.

I got to Twelve Baskets early. I took an empty table near the door and waited, somewhat afraid Stan wouldn't come. But at exactly eight o'clock, he walked in.

"Good to see you!" he said with a bright smile. "I'm starved. Let's go ahead and order."

Ricky came to our table, and Stan told him, "I'll have my usual: blueberry pancakes."

"Sounds good," I said. "I think I'll have the same."

After Ricky left with our order, Stan said, "So how are you? And what have you been doing since we were last together?"

"I've really been anticipating our time together," I began. "I've spent a lot of time praying and listening. All of that was pretty new to me. There are many things I'm looking forward to talking about. And I want you to know I feel really fortunate to be able to spend time with a mature Christian."

Stan held up his hand and said, "Hold on a minute."

Somewhat taken aback, I said "Did I say something wrong?"

"No, not really wrong, but I think your perspective may be a bit off."

"How so?" I asked.

"Rather than mature Christian," Stan replied, "I prefer to say maturing Christian. Mature suggests there's no further growing to be done. I'm convinced that maturing as a Christian is a life-long process that isn't intended by God to stop until I have taken my last breath on this side of eternity."

"And getting on the train?"

"Exactly!" Stan said. "I believe that if I ever get to the point of thinking I'm spiritually mature, I will be on the wrong path and even going backwards. There will always be more to learn about God, and there will always be more to apply to my life."

"I'm sorry I misspoke," I said.

"Nothing to apologize about," Stan replied. "Many people describe themselves or others as mature Christians. It may just be my personal quirk, but I'm convinced I'm right, and I want us to be on the same page from the beginning."

By then, Ricky returned with our breakfast, and Stan said, "Let me give thanks to God for this wonderful meal that has been provided, along with the time we will have together."

Bible verses to consider:

I say to every person among you not to think more highly of yourself than you ought to think. Romans 12:3.

And we proclaim Him, admonishing every man and teaching every man with all wisdom, that we may present every man complete in Christ. Colossians 1:28.

Work out your salvation with fear and trembling; for it is God who is at work in you, both to will and to work for His good pleasure. Philippians 2:12-13.

Prayer: Thank you, Father, for wanting me to grow in my relationship with you. Thank you for providing the Holy Spirit to help with my spiritual maturity. Thank you, too, that you allow me to pursue knowing you and your Son while you keep me on this side of eternity. I confess I often choose not to pursue knowing you more deeply, because I choose to do something different apart from you. Please forgive me. And please, Father, help me to follow every step of your lead in seeking an ever-deepening relationship with you, pursuing the maturity you intend for me. Thank you I can and do bring these prayers before you in the name of Jesus. Amen.

Think on this: Do you agree that spiritual maturity is to be pursued throughout our lives? Why or why not? If yes, what does that look like to you? Do you think you can do it on your own? Why or why not? If no, where does the help come from? Where are you in the pursuit of spiritual maturity? If you consider yourself to be spiritually mature already, do you see any danger in that? Why or why not?

DAY 7

Praying in His Name

"Stan," I began one morning, "I have a question for you."

"What's that?" he replied.

"Each time we have a meal together, you pray before we eat," I said, "and you always end your prayer saying something like "in the name of Jesus.' What's that all about?"

"Well," he replied, "I think there are several possible answers to that good question. And while most people end their prayers with 'in Jesus' name,' it may well be how some prayers should begin. But let's talk first about what it doesn't mean."

"Why start there?" I asked.

"I think it opens the path to see what it does mean. It isn't some sort of magic wand I wave over the prayer to make sure it happens, or some mystical incantation, or a signal that the prayer is over."

"Okay," I said, "that's what praying in Jesus' name is <u>not</u>. How about what it <u>is</u>?"

"First is the truth that I cannot work my way to heaven," Stan said, "or into the presence of God the Father. That is not possible. I can't come before Him on my own merits. I'm not worthy to do that. I can only approach Him through the righteousness and merits of His Son. And when I accepted God's free and gracious provision of salvation through the life, death, and resurrection of Jesus, I was granted the righteousness of Jesus, both for when I step into eternity and while I'm kept on this side."

"So," I said, "when God looks at you, it's like He sees Jesus. Is that right?"

"Yes," Stan replied. "And it's the same thing with my prayers. When I pray in Jesus' name, God hears my prayers because of Jesus, not because of me apart from Him. It's like saying to the Father, 'I'm here because of your Son, and I come in His name.' So I pray in the name of Jesus. And sometimes," he added, "it seems appropriate for me to acknowledge that fact at the beginning of my prayer, rather than at the end. But the Father knows my heart."

Bible verses to consider:
And whatever you ask in My name, that will I do, that the Father may be glorified in the Son. If you ask anything in My name, I will do it. John 14:13-14.

I am the way, and the truth, and the life; no one comes to the Father, but through Me. John 14:6.

Prayer: Thank you, Father, that I can come before you in the name of your Son because of His finished work on the cross. Thank you that He opened the way to you. Please lead me in all my prayers so that I pray only in accord with your will, His will, and the will of the Holy Spirit so that you will hear my prayers in the way they are presented—in the name of Jesus. Thank you I can and do bring these prayers before you in His glorious name. Amen.

Think on this: Have you accepted God's free and gracious gift of salvation and redemption through Christ's finished work on the cross? If no, why? If you do have the assurance of salvation, how would you explain to someone the truth that you can come before God the Father in prayer only because of what Jesus did through His life, death, and resurrection? Are you confident in that truth? Why or why not?

DAY 8

It's All About Relationship

"You seem kind of distracted this morning," said Stan. "Is everything okay?"

"You're pretty perceptive," I replied. "Yes, there's something on my mind, something that's bothering me."

"Want to talk about it?" he asked.

"I do," I said. "Last night I ran into a friend of mine who said he'd heard that I had become really religious. He seemed to be making fun of me, and I was hurt."

Stan nodded sympathetically, so I went on. "I couldn't describe what I know is happening to me, how everything about my life is changing. I tried explaining that I now have a personal relationship with God, in and through Christ. That it's not a religion, but a relationship which has changed and is changing me. But I didn't get the words out very well, and I don't think my friend had any idea what I was talking about. I was feeling pretty low when I left him, and I'm still feeling kind of down this morning."

"It's not unusual when others don't understand," Stan replied. "I've experienced the same thing. In fact, before I came to understand it myself, I had no idea there was a difference between a religion and a relationship."

"What did you come to understand?" I asked.

He said, "You see, a person who has not received the Holy Spirit just doesn't have the capacity to experience, let alone understand, the difference between a religion and a relationship. Your friend is probably thinking you've become some sort of 'holier-than-thou' person and will sit in judgment of him. The truth is that you're now allowing God to have access to every part of your life, building the relationship He has for you. What your friend can't understand," Stan continued, "is this: with a religion, a person is trying to do something to please God, but with a relationship, God is doing what He wants in and through the person who has asked Him to do that."

"Where," I asked, "does the capacity to understand the difference come from?"

"Without the Holy Spirit, who is also known as the Helper, the Counselor, and the Spirit of truth, it's impossible to understand that sort of relationship. And, because of the separation caused by our sin, it's impossible to have that kind of relationship with God until we recognize our need for Him."
"So how am I supposed to respond to someone like my friend who not only doesn't understand, but doesn't seem to have the capacity to understand?"

"Love him and be gentle," Stan replied. "Make him curious about why you are so different from who and what you used to be. Do that by relying on God. Be gentle and get your feelings of self out of the way, so the Holy Spirit is able to do His work in and through you."

As we finished our breakfast, Stan said, "Hang in there with your friend. God may very well have a life-changing and eternal impact on him through you!"

Bible verses to consider:
And I will ask the Father, and He will give you another Helper, that He may be with you forever; that is the Spirit of truth, whom the world cannot receive, because it does not behold Him or know Him, but you know Him because He abides with you, and will be in you. John 14:16-17.

And when He had said this, He breathed on them, and said to them, "Receive the Holy Spirit." John 20:22.

A gentle answer turns away wrath, but a harsh word stirs up anger. Proverbs 15:1.

Prayer: Thank you, Father, for wanting to have a personal relationship with me. Thank you for how you want me to see Christianity, not as a religion of do's and don't's, but as a relationship where I can come to you and ask, "What do you have for me to be and do, for as long as you keep me on this side of eternity?" I confess that too often I do not pursue the relationship you have for me, because I choose to go my own way. Please forgive me. And please, Father, help me to follow every step of your lead into an ever-deeper and ever-closer relationship with you, in every aspect of my life. Thank you I can and do bring these prayers before you in the name of Jesus. Amen.

Think on this: Religion or relationship? How do you look at yourself and God? Are you doing or not doing certain things because you think that is what you are supposed to do (or not do)? Or are you in a personal relationship with God where you can talk with Him about what He has for you to be and to do? These are two opposite views. What do they look like to you? Where do you want to be? How are you going to get there?

DAY 9

Like Talking to a Rock

"Yesterday," Stan began, "one of my neighbors came over, and we were talking about the importance of listening."

"That's always an important subject," I said.

"It is," Stan replied. "It seems my neighbor and his wife have been thinking about taking a trip next summer. Apparently, his wife was talking to him about ideas she had. But he was distracted by something unimportant and wasn't listening to her."

"Sounds like trouble brewing," I said.

"Exactly," Stan replied. "My neighbor said his wife decided to make a point to see if he was listening."

"How so?" I asked.

"She said, 'Let's book the train to Honolulu from Los Angeles.' And as he nodded in agreement, she laughed and said, 'I knew you weren't listening!' She then told him that talking to him sometimes felt like talking to a rock. Also, that going on vacation with an actual rock might be more enjoyable than going with him."

"I bet that got his attention!" I said.

"Big time," Stan replied. "My neighbor said he apologized, she forgave him, and they were finally able to enjoy planning the trip. Later I was thinking about my neighbor's story, and the Holy Spirit spoke up and said the same thing to me."

"What same thing?" I asked.

"Talking with me sometimes is just like talking to a rock,' Stan replied. "I don't listen to the Holy Spirit because I'm too busy being distracted by what I want to focus on. And what I want to focus on is always, always, a whole lot less important than what the Holy Spirit has for me."

"Well," I responded, "if you don't listen to the Holy Spirit, it is possible He will pack up and go on a trip without you?"

"I don't think so," Stan said, "but I sure don't want to find out!"

Bible verses to consider:
And a voice came out of the cloud, saying, "This is My Son, My Chosen One; listen to Him." Luke 9:35.

Now we have received, not the spirit of the world, but the Spirit who is from God, that we might know the things freely given to us by God, which things we also speak, not in words taught by human wisdom, but in those taught by the Spirit, combining spiritual thoughts with spiritual words. 1 Corinthians 2:12-13.

Prayer: Thank you, Father, for allowing me to listen to you through the voice of the Holy Spirit. I confess I often fail to listen to you because I choose to do something else. Please forgive me for all my attention on things other than you. Open me to want to hear everything you have for me. Help me make you the number one priority in my life so I choose to listen to you in whatever way you speak to me. Thank you I can and do bring these prayers before you in the name of Jesus. Amen.

Think on this: Have you ever experienced trying to talk to someone who only pretended to be listening? If so, how did that make you feel? How do you think the Holy Spirit feels when we purposefully choose not to listen to Him? Is listening to the Holy Spirit a problem for you? Why or why not? If a person stops listening to the voice of the Holy Spirit, do you think a time will come when the Holy Spirit stops talking to that person? Why or why not?

DAY 10

The Journal of The Journey

"Stan," I said, "when we first got together, you indicated it took a long time to develop a growing relationship with God. Will you tell me more about that?"

"Be happy to," he replied. "When I first became a Christian (in other words got my ticket to glory) it was difficult for me to spend daily, regular time with God. I had been told it was essential, but it just didn't happen for me. I tried and tried, but nothing seemed to work. I knew I was a Christian, but I also knew I was experiencing a very shallow type of Christianity. I had been converted, I had my ticket, but I had not started the process of being transformed. It was like I was stuck on conversion."

"Stuck on conversion? How so?"

"Well," Stan said, "I was attending a good church weekly and had Christian friends. I would spend some time praying. I was involved in a Bible study and occasionally would read a daily devotional. But I was feeling real empty. It felt like nothing was happening, because, in fact, nothing was happening. I was not moving toward transformation. I simply was not growing as a Christian."

"So what changed?" I asked.

"A friend suggested I start journaling, a written conversation with God. I wasn't sure what that meant, but I tried it. After a day or two, I'd make the next entry weeks later. I started the same process several times and failed. It just didn't work for me. It seemed I couldn't have a regular time with God each day."

"I assume you had a breakthrough at some point," I said. "How did it happen?"

"I read a book by my pastor," Stan said. "It wasn't specifically about journaling, but it got me started."

"How so?" I ask.

"In one part of the book," Stan replied, "my pastor suggested that a good way to develop a regular devotion time with God was by reading the fifteenth chapter of John's Gospel every day for thirty days, asking God each day how He wanted me to grow."

"What's so special about that chapter?" I asked.

"John 15 is sometimes called the "Vine and branches" chapter. It's where Jesus says He is the vine, His Father is the vinedresser, and we are the branches. We are to abide in the vine. The idea of abiding in the vine is very important. We'll talk about that, probably more than once."

"Did you do what the pastor suggested?" I asked.

"I did," said Stan. "I read the fifteenth chapter of John every morning and prayed. To my amazement, I kept it up day after day, for about two weeks."

"After those two weeks," he continued, "I began to write what I sensed God was telling me from those verses. I would write questions and answers. I would write about things I was concerned about. I wrote prayers. Again, to my utter amazement, it was the beginning of daily journaling that has now gone on for many years."

"Wow!" I responded. "All that happened because you read John fifteen?

"Exactly," Stan said. "After thirty days, I went on to chapter sixteen, and on to the end of John's gospel. Then I finished the rest of the New Testament. After that I began with the first book of the Bible, the Old Testament book of Genesis."

"Always journaling?" I asked.

"Yes," Stan replied. "And God has been amazingly faithful over the years in giving me insight into what He has for me to see and learn."

"That's quite a journey!" I exclaimed.

"Well put, my friend," Stan replied. "That's exactly what I call my journal, now dozens and dozens of volumes. I call it The Journal of the Journey."

"I would like to know more about this," I said.

"Journaling is a real passion for me. It's been my way of relating to God ever more deeply. For me there's something very special connecting my mind, spirit, hand, pen, and paper. I know journaling isn't for everyone, and it may not be for you, but I will be happy to tell you more from time to time, if you're interested."

"I would like that," I responded.

"Okay, I'll make a note of it," Stan said with a smile.

Bible verses to consider:
And in the early morning, while it was still dark, He arose and went out and departed to a lonely place, and was praying there. Mark 1:35.

I will meditate on Your precepts and regard Your ways. I shall delight in Your statues; I will not forget Your word. Psalm 119:15-16.

Prayer: Thank you, Father, for wanting us to have an ever-deepening relationship through spending time together. I confess there are too many times when I do not want to spend time with you, because I choose to spend the time on something else. Please forgive me. And please help me follow every step of your lead into as deep a relationship as possible this side of eternity. Father, I know you want to spend time with me. Please strengthen my desire to spend time with you. Thank you I can and do bring these prayers before you in the name of Jesus. Amen.

Think on this: Spending time with God is essential for a deepening relationship. Journaling is one way to spend that time. Have you tried journaling? Did you give up on it? If so, try what Stan suggests, and focus on a narrow part of Scripture. The fifteenth chapter of John's gospel is a great place to start. Read it and write to God about it. See what happens. It may make a lasting difference in your faith walk!

DAY 11

Contentment Realized

Stan startled me one morning at breakfast by suddenly asking, "Are you content?"

"Content about what?" I asked.

"Everything and anything," he replied.

"I don't know," I responded. "I don't think much about that. Why do you ask?"

"I think it's a really important subject," he replied. "For a long time, I had the wrong perception of being content. I considered it to be settling for second best."

"Second best? What do you mean?"

"Like saying, 'Oh well, I'll just have to be content until I get what I want.' But one day, while I was journaling and praying, it became real clear to me that contentment is actually the height of what God has for me. Not something less than that. Knowing all that God has for me, and pursuing it, tops everything! If I'm fully surrendered to all God has and wants for me on this side of eternity, I'll be absolutely content. No second best!"

"Have you ever felt discontent in your relationship with God?" I asked.

"I know all about discontentment," he said, "and I can assure you it isn't from God. Such discontentment is the fruit of the world, the flesh, and the devil, along with a good dose of self."

"It's real easy for me to get pulled down by discontentment, but it doesn't have to be that way. I believe it's essential not to focus on short-term fulfillment that will turn into long-term emptiness. No, I have to keep the proper perspective, focusing on the fulfillment God gives, both long-term and short-term."

"Which is which?" I asked.

"The first perspective is long-term, very long-term. Eternal. Spending all eternity in God's presence when this life is over. The second perspective is only possible with the first."

"Okay, then what is second?" I asked.

"Knowing I am in the care of Almighty God," Stan replied, "and being used for His purposes while He keeps me on this side of eternity. That, I believe, is true, divinely-granted contentment."

Bible verses to consider:
I have learned to be content in whatever circumstances I am in. Philippians 4:11.

And others are the ones on whom seed was sown among the thorns; these are the ones who have heard the word, and the worries of the world, and the deceitfulness of riches, and desires for other things enter in and choke the word and it becomes unfruitful. Mark 4:18-19.

Prayer: Thank you, Father, for the gift of absolute contentment in life eternally with you when it is time. Thank you, too, for showing me that the height of contentment in this life is found in a relationship with you, where I am who you intend. I confess that too often I am discontent because I want my own way. Please forgive me. Help me follow every step of your lead, exactly as you intend, knowing contentment now flows from the assurance of being in your eternal presence when it's time. Thank you I can and do bring these prayers before you in the name of Jesus. Amen.

Think on this: Are you content in the knowledge you will spend eternity in God's presence when it is time? If no, why? Do you know how to have that contentment? Are you content with your life? Why or why not? Are you content in your relationship with God? If no, what needs to be changed? If yes, do you think your contentment is the kind that God wants to give you? What does it take to get there? To stay there?

DAY 12

Choosing to Draw Closer to God

One morning Stan was back on the subject of journaling.

"I was making my way through the Bible," he said, "going through a chapter each day. I went through the Book of Acts and then the various letters, sensing something really special was happening to me. But I just couldn't put my finger on it. Have you ever had that kind of feeling?"

"I know exactly what you're talking about," I said. "Happens all the time."

"I had this wonderful sense of being ever closer to God, but not knowing why. And then one morning, when I was reading the letter the apostle James wrote, it all made sense."

"How so?" I asked. "What did you read?"

"The verse that almost jumped off the page at me," Stan replied, "was James 4:8. 'Draw near to God and He will draw near to you.' It was like James had written specifically to me, because that was exactly what I was experiencing. As I deliberately chose to draw closer to God, He responded in a magnificent manner. Can you imagine? The Lord God of the universe choosing to draw closer to me?"

"That is amazing," I said. "Tell me more."

"As God draws closer to me, and as I again choose to draw closer to Him, He responds. And round and round it goes. Closer and closer we get. And deeper and deeper our relationship grows! It's a precious circle of drawing ever closer. It was and is beyond my wildest dreams."

"Does that sort of thing happen with every believer?" I asked.

"I think that's the plan," Stan replied. "I also think that, for whatever reason, not every Christian chooses to take steps in that direction. And I always have to remember it's an ongoing choice. It does not and will not happen automatically. God does not force Himself on anyone. But if a person has the genuine desire to know Him, and chooses to draw near to Him, that person better get ready for something very wonderful to happen!"

Bible verse to consider:
Draw near to God and he will draw near to you. James 4:8.

Prayer: Thank you, Father, for drawing ever closer to me when I first chose to draw closer to you. Thank you, too, that you continue to draw ever closer in response to my choice in that direction. I confess too often I do not choose to draw close to you, but I choose to draw closer to myself or to other things apart from you. Please forgive the foolishness of not wanting to be ever closer to you. And please, Father, help me follow every step of your lead into the deepest possible relationship with you. Thank you I can and do bring these prayers before you in the name of Jesus. Amen.

Think on this: Are you as close to God as you want to be? As close as He wants you to be? Do you believe that if you choose to draw closer to God, He will respond by drawing closer to you? If no, why? If so, what does that kind of closeness look like? If you want to be closer to God, what will it take for that to happen?

DAY 13

Why Hurry through the Bible?

"Stan," I began, "you've talked about 'spiritual journaling' and its impact on your faith walk. I have a question about that."

"What's on your mind?" Stan replied. "I'm happy to talk about most anything you want to talk about."

"You said you started with the fifteenth chapter of John's gospel and then read on. How much did you read each day?"

"For quite a while," he said, "every day I read one chapter from the New Testament and one from the Old Testament."

"And you were writing in your journal about each chapter?"

"I was," Stan said. "But it didn't take God very long to show me He had something else in mind for me."

"Something else?" I asked. "What?"

"I was very excited about what I was doing with the journaling," Stan responded. "I sensed I was really on to something as a way to draw closer to God. I told everyone who would listen. It was, for me, an experience I wanted for everyone. I'm afraid I may have bored more than a few people with my enthusiasm! Thankfully, a friend was kind enough to send me a book that changed my entire focus."

"In what way?" I asked.

"Well," Stan replied, "one of the author's nuggets of wisdom was to stay with a particular Bible verse until I was satisfied I'd claimed all that it had to offer. Suddenly it became very clear to me I was probably missing important things by reading whole chapters each day."

"Kind of like driving someplace," I replied, "without stopping to enjoy the scenery."

"Exactly," said Stan. "Or without taking time to stop and smell the magnificent roses of God's word! With this whole idea of slowing down, I think it was the voice of God speaking through the Holy Spirit saying, in essence, 'What's the hurry?' I was shown I had the wrong focus. I was missing the point."

"What point?" I asked.

"It became clear to me," Stan replied, "the point wasn't to get through the Bible; the point was to see and learn what the Bible has for me, verse by verse."

"So did you slow down?"

"I did," Stan replied. "And I can say slowing down has made a huge difference for me in the process of drawing closer to God. Many days I focus on a single verse, and some verses get more than one day!"

"God's word is rich," he continued. "It's like digging for golden nuggets. I don't want to miss any truth he has for my, by digging too quickly. I want to discover and own those nuggets by making them a part of my life!"

"Obviously," I responded, "at that rate it takes you a long time to get through the Bible."

"You're right, my friend," Stan responded. "But there's always the question 'What's the hurry?'

"What do you think I will do when I get to the end of the Bible again?"

"Start over!"

"Exactly," Stan said. "God will keep me here on this side of eternity for as long as He wants. And I believe He wants my Bible to be open until the moment when it's time for me to board the train!"

Bible verses to consider:
So faith comes from hearing, and hearing by the word of Christ. Romans 10:17.

All Scripture is inspired by God and profitable for teaching, for reproof, for correction, for training in righteousness; that the man of God may be adequate, equipped for every good work. 2 Timothy 3:16-17.

Prayer: Thank you, Father, that your precious word is available for me to read and focus upon, so that I will know you and your Son as well as possible. I confess I too often rush through your word and miss what you have for me to see, learn, and make part of my life. Please forgive me. And please help me to focus on, understand, receive, and embrace every thought you have for me, from every verse you put before me. Please help me not to rush and miss any part of what you say. Thank you I can and do bring these prayers before you in the name of Jesus. Amen.

Think on this: How do you approach reading God's word? Do you simply read, or do you search for all God has for you, to know Him more deeply? Why is the Bible called the "living word?" Are you satisfied with how you approach reading it? Why or why not? What would it look like for you to search God's word for more meaningful applications? What things can you think of that would help you?

DAY 14

What's that Funny Noise?

"One of my neighbors stopped by last night, in a car I hadn't seen before," Stan began. "Turns out it was a rental."

"Why a rental car?" I asked. "Something happen to his?"

"He said his own car was making a funny noise," Stan replied, "so he took it to Mike's Auto Repair."

"Mike is real good at fixing most anything," I said.

"Yes he is," Stan replied. "My neighbor said Mike listened to the engine for just a few seconds. Then he checked the oil level. He asked my neighbor how long it had been since he last checked the oil level. It seems there was hardly any oil in the engine, which had caused a lot of damage. The funny noise wasn't so funny after all!"

"I check the oil level just about every time I fill the car with gas," I said.

"Me, too," Stan replied. "But my neighbor couldn't say how long it had been for him."

"That oversight is probably going to cost him a bundle," I said.

"Mike is reasonable," Stan replied, "but I'm sure it will cost a lot more than my neighbor wants to pay. His situation reminded me of myself, when I go too long without checking the level of the Holy Spirit filling my life."

"Checking the level? Is that really necessary?"

"Very definitely," Stan replied. "I learned a long time ago, if I don't check for leakage and don't keep myself filled with the presence of the Holy Spirit, I am headed for a breakdown in my relationship with God and also my relationships with other people."

"How do you check for leakage?" I asked.

"Look at what's going on in my life," Stan replied. "Examine my relationship with God and my faith walk. Check how receptive I am to the voice of the Holy Spirit, and check if I am manifesting His fruit."

"That's a lot of checking," I said.

"It may sound like it," Stan replied, "but not really. If I am continually open to the leading of the Holy Spirit, He will reveal any damage that needs attention. If I go too long without some serious self-examination, my life may become like my neighbor's car: making funny noises that really aren't that funny!"

Bible verses to consider:
Be filled with the Spirit. Ephesians 5:18.

But the fruit of the Spirit is love, joy, peace, patience, kindness, goodness, faithfulness, gentleness, self-control. Galatians 5:22-23.

Prayer: Thank you, Father, for your presence in me through the Holy Spirit. Too often I neglect to examine my life for evidence that I am full, even overflowing, with His presence. I confess those failings and ask for your forgiveness. I ask for help to follow your lead, so that I can continually experience His presence and manifest His fruit in every aspect of my life. Thank you I can and do bring these prayers before you in the name of Jesus. Amen.

Think on this: What does it mean to be "filled with the Spirit?" Have you ever felt like you were "running on empty"? Do you know how to measure His presence in and through your life? If so, what does that measuring look like? How often do you do that measuring? Is it something that has to be consciously measured? Why or why not?

DAY 15

Whose Mark is That?

As we were finishing our blueberry pancakes, Stan asked, "Do you play golf?"

"I do," I said. "I really enjoy it, but I'm not very good."

"You just described my game," Stan said with a laugh. "Can I tell you about a valuable lesson I learned through playing golf with a friend?"

"Go ahead," I said eagerly.

"His name was Dick, a dear friend who boarded the train a few years ago. I sure do miss him! We played a lot of golf together. At first, neither of us would mark our ball to be able to identify which was which. But whenever we were looking in the rough, and found a ball, Dick would say, 'I think that's probably the one I hit.' But we were never sure, and since it was a friendly game, I didn't question Dick. But just to keep it clear, I started putting my initial on my own ball, to make sure I was hitting the right one."

"And avoiding the penalty for hitting the wrong one," I added.

"That's right. And as time passed, I changed my mark to a cross. Because I believe that putting Christ in place of me is the essence of Christianity, changing my mark from my initial to a cross seemed like a good move."

"Like what?" I asked.

"When I stand over my ball for my next shot and see the cross, it certainly puts my focus on the right thing, which is to represent Christ on the golf course. And there have been many times when someone I am playing with has asked why I mark my ball with a cross. That's opened up opportunities to share the truth of the cross."

"That's a great thing to happen on the course," I said.

"Definitely," said Stan. "Golfing with Dick gave me what I call 'the theology of the golf ball.' It opened up a lot of thought about marking every area of my life with the cross, so others see a difference and perhaps wonder what motivates me. Then I can share what can also change their lives and eternal destinations. As for you, my friend," Stan concluded, "I encourage you to think about what parts of your life can and should be marked with the cross."

"How do I do that?" I asked.

"For me," Stan replied, "it's to deliberately focus on areas of my life that don't yet manifest the life God has for me. I dedicate those areas specifically to God, for whatever He wants to do in and through me. It's like letting God put His mark on me. I am identified and identifiable as belonging to Him. This whole subject is the crucial center of being a Christian. It's called discipleship."

"Discipleship?" I replied. "Not sure I know about that."

"We will definitely spend more time talking about it," Stan said. "For now, you should know that it basically involves three steps."

"What three steps?" I asked.

"Denying what I want to do apart from God, doing whatever God has for me to do, and following Him wherever He wants to lead."

"Discipleship in three easy steps,' I responded. "I'll look forward to that."

"They're not so easy," Stan said with smile, "but I suspect we will have some good discussions as we go down the discipleship path together."

Bible verses to consider:
If anyone wishes to come after Me, let him deny himself, and take up his cross daily, and follow Me. Luke 9:23.

Or do you not know that your body is a temple of the Holy Spirit who is in you, whom you have from God, and that you are not your own? For you have been bought with a price; therefore glorify God in your body. 1 Corinthians 6:19-20.

Prayer: Thank you, Father, for every learning opportunity you present to me. Thank you for the people you bring into my life to teach me. Please help me discern what you want me to learn, and help me apply it to my life. I confess that too often I do not see and do not learn. Please forgive me. And please, Father, help me follow every step of your lead so I am only who you intend, seeking to do your will, in every aspect of my life, wherever I might be. Thank you I can and do bring these prayers before you in the name of Jesus. Amen.

Think on this: God wants to manifest His presence in our lives wherever we are, whatever we are doing. Is that a consistent part of your life? Why or why not? Are there areas in your life God wants to "mark" for Himself? What will that look like? In the verses above from 1 Corinthians, what do you think it means that "you have been bought with a price?" What was the price and who paid it?

DAY 16

Are You Listening?

"That breakfast must taste awfully good today," said Stan. "It seems to have all your attention."

"Sorry," I replied. "It does taste as good as ever, but actually my mind was wandering. I admit I wasn't listening to you. Really sorry!"

"That's okay," Stan responded. "I also have a tendency to let my mind wander. I just try to be careful not to let it wander too far. You know," he added, "the whole subject of wandering reminds me of a line from J.R.R. Tolkien's book *The Fellowship of the Ring*: 'Not all those who wander are lost.'"

"Do you agree with that?" I asked.

"Well," Stan replied, "I think it depends on who is wandering where, and why they are wandering. I myself have certainly wandered in ways that showed I was lost. Before I became a Christian, I was certainly wandering as a lost person. I was lost for eternity and didn't even know it. And even as a Christian, I have a tendency to wander away from God, doing what I want to do, when and where I please."

"Any chance that kind of wandering can make you lost in the eternal sense?" I asked.

"No," Stan replied. "Not possible, because I have the assurance of salvation that comes from God's grace through the life, death, and resurrection of Jesus. I accepted that, and I'm ready to step into eternity because I know where I'm going. However," he continued, "wandering around on my own this side of eternity can certainly make me lost, in the sense of not being where God wants me to be."

"I sure don't want that to happen to me," I said.

"Neither do I," Stan responded. "That's why I'm glad we can enjoy breakfast together—and more importantly, talk about following the One who wants to lead us."

Bible verses to consider:
With all my heart I have sought you; do not let me wander from your commandments. Psalm 119:10.

All of us like sheep have gone astray, each of us has turned to his own way; but the Lord has caused the iniquity of us to fall on Him. Isaiah 53:6.

Prayer: Thank you, Father, for saving me from being lost for eternity, through the finished work of Christ's cross. You saved me from endless wandering apart from you. I also thank you for wanting to lead and keep me from wandering away on this side of eternity. I confess that too many times I want to go my own way. Please forgive all those wanderings. I ask you to lead and help me deny myself, take up what you have for me to take up, and truly follow you so that I keep from wandering away on my own. Thank you I can and do bring these prayers before you in the name of Jesus. Amen.

Think on this: Do you tend to wander? If yes, what does that wandering look like? Are you secure in knowing you will not spend eternity wandering apart from the presence of God? If no, talk with your pastor right away. If you have the assurance of eternity with God when it is time, how about wandering away from Him on this side of eternity? Is that a struggle for you? If so, what can you do about it? What does it look like to stay close to God?

DAY 17

Cultivating Hard Ground

"I don't know if I mentioned it before," Stan began, "but I grew up on a farm. My dad grew wheat, barley, and oats. He was a good farmer."

"I don't know much about farming," I said. "I grew up in a city."

"Farming can be a tough way to make a living," Stan said, "especially the way my dad did it."

"How so?" I asked.

"He was what's called a 'dry-land farmer'," Stan replied, "which means there was no irrigation. All of the needed moisture had to come from the sky, as God's provision. Some years there was plenty of moisture, and the crops were good. Some years were too dry. But regardless of the amount of moisture, the ground had to be cultivated every year. The soil had to be prepared for the seeds to be planted. That meant plowing and breaking up the hard ground so the seeds could sprout and grow."

"Were there times when the seeds didn't produce anything?" I asked.

"Not too often," Stan replied, "because, like I said, my dad was a good farmer. But there were other farmers who did not do what was required to produce a good crop. What their farms yielded was often less than my dad's."

"I didn't expect to learn about farming today," I said with a smile.

Stan returned my smiled and then grew serious. "My father was not a believer, so I wasn't raised with a Christian foundation. But now that I am pursuing transformation, I can see that there is a lot of similarity between growing crops and growing in the Christian faith."

"How so?" I asked.

"We all have hearts that can be like hard ground," Stan said. "Hard hearts toward God are part of the natural human condition. But it doesn't have to be that way. Our hearts can be cultivated so we are receptive to the seeds God wants to plant in us, the seeds of His will. Depending on how I choose to cultivate my heart for such seeds, they may or may not grow."

"So," I responded, "it's possible to produce no crop, a little crop, or an abundant crop from what is planted in the heart. Is that the point?"

"Exactly," Stan said. "How a person cultivates the natural hardness of the heart determines what and how much spiritual fruit is produced in that person's life."

"How do you cultivate your heart?" I asked.

"Good question," he said. "I can choose to cultivate my heart by knowing God's word and absorbing it into my mind. If I don't give attention to God's voice as I meditate and pray, my heart's soil will remain hard."

"This farming analogy is really eye-opening for me," I said.

"I agree," said Stan. "I've thought a lot about dad's work, as I've considered the Christian life. It's all a matter of choosing to get out of God's way so what He wants will be planted, and will sprout, grow, and produce an abundant harvest."

"I may be wrong," I said, "but this seems like a really big subject."

"Oh, it's a big subject all right. And it's not learned in a day or a week, but in a lifetime. I believe cultivating hard hearts is the center of true Christian discipleship. Jesus spent a lot of time talking about it. We, too, will spend a lot of time on it because it's so important. But for the moment, get the picture clear in your mind."

"What picture?" I asked.

"We all have hearts that need to be cultivated to break up their hardness," Stan replied, "but God has prepared and provided everything needed for that cultivation. I just have to choose to use what God has for me: knowing His word and listening to His voice."

Bible verses to consider:

Sow with a view to righteousness, reap in accord with kindness; break up your fallow ground, for it is time to seek the Lord until He comes to rain righteousness on you. Hosea 10:12

He who sows righteousness gets a true reward. Proverbs 11:18.

This I say therefore, and affirm together with the Lord, that you walk no longer just as the Gentiles also walk, in the futility of their mind, being darkened in their understanding, excluded from the life of God, because of the ignorance that is in them, because of the hardness of their heart; and they, having become callous, have given themselves over to sensuality, or the practice of every kind of impurity with greediness. Ephesians 4:17-19.

Prayer: Father, you are well acquainted with the hardness of my heart that exists apart from you. I confess that way too often I do not seek to break up that hardness because I choose to go my own way apart from you. Please forgive me for neglecting what you have provided to break up the hardness of my heart. I ask you to plant, grow, and reap all you want in and through me. I choose to accept all your provision. Please, Father, break up that hard soil, plant your seeds, and cause them to grow exactly as you want. Thank you I can and do bring these prayers before you in the name of Jesus. Amen.

Think on this: What does it look like to have a hard heart towards God? Is your heart hard or soft? Somewhere in between, depending on circumstances you face? Perhaps you have never tried to plant seeds in hard ground, but can you imagine trying to plant them in an asphalt street? Impossible? Examine your heart to see if it is sufficiently cultivated for God's purposes. If no, what can be done? Do you want to do that? Why or why not?

DAY 18

Mind the Gap

Ricky had just refilled our coffee cups when Stan said, "A few years ago, my wife and I were blessed to be able to spend time in London."

"High on my list of places I want to go," I replied. "Did you enjoy it?"

"We had a fabulous time," Stan said. "We almost wore ourselves out trying to see all there was to see. It's a big place! We took just about every mode of transportation available, but the one we liked best was the underground. We could get all around London quickly, at a reasonable cost. But the first time we were on the underground, there was something we couldn't understand."

"What was that?"

"Every time the train door opened, a recorded announcement played over the public address system. But we had no clue what it was saying. Finally I asked a fellow sitting next to us what the announcement was. He said, 'Mind the gap.' He explained that it was a warning about the space between the train car and the platform."

"Not to trip over it," I replied. "That makes sense."

"So when we got off, we noticed there were signs posted with the same warning: Mind the Gap. From then on, every time my wife and I would get ready to step on or off the train, we would warn each other, 'Mind the gap!'"

I smiled at that, and Stan said, "Before we left London for home, I bought a replica of that sign. It's on the wall of my study. It serves two purposes."

"What two purposes?"

"First," Stan replied, "the sign reminds me of our wonderful time in London. But more importantly, it warns me about the danger of stumbling.

It reminds me to look for any 'gap' between God's purposes and what I am doing in my daily life."

"Mind the gap," I said. "I can remember that!"

Bible verse to consider:
If anyone walks in the day, he does not stumble, because he sees the light of this world. John 11:9.

Prayer: Thank you, Father, for providing warning signs to keep me from stumbling. I confess that way too often I ignore your warnings and stumble, because I fail to mind the gap between who I am and who you intend me to be. Please forgive me. I thank you that when I do stumble, you are there to pick me up, dust me off, bandage my wounds, and set me back on your lighted path. Please help me heed your warnings, so you don't have to do all that! Thank you I can and do bring these prayers before you in the name of Jesus. Amen.

Think on this: Is there a gap between who you are, what you do, and what God intends for you? If so, why is that? What can be done about it? What would it look like for you to have no gaps in any area of your life? Is that possible? Why or why not?

DAY 19

Understanding the Bible—or Not

"Stan," I said, "since we've been getting together, I've spent quite a bit of time reading the Bible. I have a question."

"What's that?" Stan replied.

"Some of what I'm reading is real hard for me to understand," I said. "Do you ever have that problem?"

"First of all," Stan replied, "I want to compliment you on being serious enough about your Bible to ask the question. Secondly, let me tell you about a friend. She's a dear friend and a Christian, but she's real reluctant to read or study the Bible."

"Any particular reason?" I asked.

"She says it's too hard for her to understand," Stan replied, "so she doesn't even try."

"Doesn't even try," I repeated. "Do you think that's unusual?"

"Not at all," Stan replied. "I think it's probably fairly common. All I have to do is recall one point in my own Christian life. I didn't spend much time with the Bible."

"Any particular reason?" I asked.

"Two quick reasons," he said. "First, parts of Scripture were difficult for me to understand. But there was a bigger roadblock."

"What was that?"

"I didn't even have the desire to try to understand," Stan replied. "I didn't pursue the 'study' part of Bible study. I mainly read the Bible because I thought I was supposed to. I didn't approach it as the life-giving word of God."

"Maybe that's why I'm having the problem."

"Could be," he said. "The other day I ran across something in the apostle Peter's second letter that relates to the idea of finding parts of the Bible hard to understand."

"What's that?" I asked.

"He said, 'There are some things that are hard to understand' in Paul's letters. Other passages say something similar."

"Such as?"

"There's the account of two men on the road to Emmaus talking about how they did not understand about Jesus and why He died. And there's the account of the apostle Philip asking an Ethiopian if he understood what he was reading from the prophet Isaiah. The Ethiopian's response was, 'How can I?'"

"So it's okay to admit I don't understand parts of the Bible?"

"Of course," Stan assured me. "What is wrong is when we stop trying to understand. Or stop caring."

"How can I learn about the difficult parts of Scripture?" I asked.

"There are all sorts of resources," Stan said. "Pastors, books, fellow Christians. But I think the most important one is God Himself, in the Person of the indwelling Holy Spirit. After all, there's a good reason He's called the Helper!

Bible verses to consider:

Just as also our beloved brother Paul, according to the wisdom given him, wrote to you, as also in all his letters, speaking in them of these things, in which are some things hard to understand. 2 Peter 3:15-16.

And beginning with Moses and with all the prophets, [Jesus] explained to them the things concerning Himself in all the Scriptures. Luke 24:27.

And when Philip had run up, he heard [the Ethiopian] reading Isaiah the prophet, and said to him, "Do you understand what you are reading?" And he said, "Well, how could I, unless someone guides me?" And he invited Philip to come up and sit with him. Acts of the Apostles 8:30-31.

But the Helper, the Holy Spirit, whom the Father will send in My name, He will teach you all things, and bring to your remembrance all that I said to you. John 14:26.

Prayer: Thank you, Father, for your written word. Thank you for making it available so I can grow in my knowledge of you. You know that I find some parts difficult to understand. And I confess that there are times I stop trying to understand. Please forgive that foolishness. Help me to pursue the knowledge of you and your Son as deeply as possible on this side of eternity. Protect me from falling into Satan's trap of not seeking to know or understand. Thank you that your indwelling Holy Spirit is the Helper who gives me understanding as I study your word. Thank you I can and do bring these prayers to you in the name of Jesus. Amen.

Think on this: Do you think it is important to know God's word? Why or why not? Have you ever found something in the Bible difficult to understand? If so, what did you do about that? Give up or dig deeper? Do you agree that if reading the Bible is important, studying it is even more important? Are you involved in a formal Bible study group? If no, why? If you are not, and you want to be, do you know how to find one?

DAY 20

Be Ready to Share

"I've got another golf story for you," said Stan one morning.

"What's up?" I asked.

"I don't do it so much anymore, but I used to play with a men's group every Tuesday morning. It was a large group, and I usually didn't play with the same men every week. One morning as I was putting my bag on the cart, I saw a fellow I hadn't seen for a long time. His name was Pete. I shook his hand and asked how he was doing. He told me he had been dealing with throat cancer and hadn't been able to play golf for several months."

"Wow," I said. "How did you respond?"

"I told him it was great to see him back on the golf course. But then he told me he'd been to the doctor just the day before, and that the cancer was back. Pete said he wasn't going to pursue any further treatment. Because it had been so painful, he was not going to have radiation or chemotherapy. He said he was 'ready to go.' At first, I had nothing to say. Then the Holy Spirit whispered to my conscience, 'Are you going to speak to Pete or not?' I listened to that voice and prayed silently for a few seconds. Then I was able to get the words out."

'What did the Holy Spirit help you say?"

"I said, 'Pete, if you have decided you are ready to go, it's essential that you know where you are going when you step into eternity, and that you are satisfied with the destination.' Then I took a little booklet out of my bag; it contained the Gospel of John. I told Pete, 'This explains salvation, getting your ticket to glory and being assured of where you are going.'"

"Do you always carry those booklets with you?"

"I do. They come in real handy when the opportunity arises, as it did with Pete. We spent the rest of the day on the golf course talking about eternity, the reasons I believe, and whether or not he would be prepared when the time came."

"Did Pete receive his ticket that day?" I asked.

"I don't know that he did," Stan said. "He said he appreciated our time together and that he would give a lot of thought to our conversation. I told him I'd be praying for him, for his health and his salvation."

"Did he thank you for that, too?" I asked.

Stan nodded. "I certainly hope I'll see Pete when I step off the train into glory. But accepting salvation is a choice, and I couldn't make it for him. Each person must choose. And sharing the truth is also a choice. I'm thankful I was able to speak when the Holy Spirit prompted me. I'm grateful that He prepared me to understand and share the gospel. And I'm forever thankful that He used other believers before me, who obeyed the prompting of the Spirit and passed on the truth to me. I'm thankful they desired to obey God's voice—and I hope to do nothing less."

Bible verse to consider:
Always be ready to make a defense to every one who asks you to give an account for the hope that is in you. 1 Peter 3:15.

Prayer: Thank you, Father, for the salvation you have made available to every person, as your free and gracious gift to all who believe. Thank you for wanting me to be part of your plan by telling others about this gift. I confess that too often I do not share with others what you have for them. I do that because I am not prepared or am reluctant to step out of my comfort zone. Please forgive me. Help me be ready to make an eternal difference with each person you bring before me. I want to leave my comfort zone and be in yours. Keep me always grateful that Christians went out of their way to bring me to the truth. May I do the same for others, whenever you want. Thank you I can and do bring these prayers before you in the name of Jesus. Amen.

Think on this: If you have the assurance of salvation, it's likely because someone told you about God's provision. Where would you be if no one had told you about Christ? Are you reluctant to tell others why you have the faith you do? Reluctant to tell them they can have the same thing? If so, why? What would it look like for you to always be ready to tell others about what is freely available to them? Do you want that? Do you think God wants that? Why or why not?

DAY 21

Appointments: Divine or Mine?

"I was taught a powerful lesson yesterday," Stan began one morning.

"What was going on?" I asked.

"I had an appointment with a fellow over in Pleasanton," Stan said, "to talk about starting a new fellowship group at the church he attends."

"How'd it go?"

"Once I got there," Stan said, "it was just fine, but the lesson occurred on the way. There was some road construction near the summit that caused traffic to back up, because only one lane was open. The flagger would stop traffic until it was clear to proceed. I was stopped at the front of the line. I was feeling more than a little agitated that I was going to be late for my appointment. That's when the lesson occurred."

"What?" I asked.

"I rolled down the window and asked the flagger how long the wait would be. He told me ten or fifteen minutes. 'I hope you're not in a hurry,' he said."

"How did you respond to that?"

"I told him I'd be late getting to a church in Pleasanton. He said he lived there and asked which church. I told him the name, and he said he'd been thinking about checking that one out. He said he and his family had never attended a church, but he was feeling they should begin."

"What a coincidence!" I said.

"Not a coincidence," Stan corrected. "I believe God had a divine appointment for me with that flagger. We spent the whole fifteen minutes talking about church and the difference God had made in my life and in my eternal destination."

"Did you give him one of your booklets with John's Gospel?"

"Sure did," Stan said. "I told him it would explain God's plan of salvation and how to accept Christ. The fellow thanked me and said he'd be giving a lot of thought to what I said."

"Do you think he will become a Christian?"

"That's my prayer. But whether it happens is not up to me. My role is to be obedient, leaving the results to God."

"But you have to be ready to be obedient," I replied. "Is that the point?"

"It is. God's scheduled appointments are always a whole lot more important than mine. I just have to stop and be aware of what He has for me to do."

"Such as talking to people He brings into your life?"

"Exactly. I have to be ready when I sense God, through the Holy Spirit, speaking and asking me, 'Are you going to say or do anything here that will make a difference in this person's life now and for all eternity?' I need to be ready for all of God's appointments."

Bible verses to consider:
Now I want you to know, brethren, that my circumstances have turned out for the greater progress of the gospel. Philippians 1:12.

Always being ready to make a defense to every one who asks you to give an account for the hope that is in you, yet with gentleness and reverence. 1 Peter 3:15.

Prayer: Thank you, Father, that you have divine appointments for me that are much more important than the appointments I make for myself. You know, and I know, how many times I fail to pay attention to the appointments you have for me. Please forgive those times I prioritize what I want over what you want. Please open me to see everything in my circumstances in light of your kingdom purposes. Thank you I can and do bring all of these prayers before you in the name of Jesus. Amen.

Think on this: Have you ever had a divine appointment? If so, what happened? Have you ever missed an opportunity for that kind of appointment? If so, why? What would it look like if you were continually open to the appointments God may have for you?

DAY 22

Call it What it is: Disobedience

Ricky took our breakfast orders and briskly moved on.

"Ricky is a great employee," Stan said. "Always reliable. But imagine what could happen if the cook wasn't."

"What's on your mind?" I asked.

"Say we wait for forty-five minutes, and no breakfast comes. Then we ask Ricky why he hasn't brought it. Imagine if he says, 'I put in the order, but the cook said he'll prepare it when he gets around to it.'"

"Sounds like we'd go hungry," I laughed.

Stan laughed, too, then grew serious. "How long do you think the cook would have his job? Or, if he stayed around with that attitude, how long would this place stay in business?"

"Probably not very long," I said.

"I think you're right," he said. "So consider this question: how deep do you think my relationship with God will get if I say, 'I haven't obeyed yet, but I will when I get around to it'?"

"Same sort of answer," I replied. "Not very deep."

"Exactly, my friend," Stan said. "Ricky can't deliver our breakfast if the cook hasn't prepared it. The cook saying he'll fix our breakfast is not the same as fixing it. God wants my obedience. But saying I'll obey is not obeying. Obedience to God deepens my relationship with Him, and I can guarantee that if I choose not to obey Him, the chances of a deepening relationship are somewhere between nil and zero!"

"And what can get in the way of obedience?" I asked.

"Being shortsighted and caring more about myself and what I want to do, instead of what God has for me to do."

"As simple as that? I asked.

"Yes," Stan replied. "As simple, and as complicated, as not calling failure to obey what it is: disobedience."

Bible verses to consider:
If you love Me, you will keep my commandments. John 14:15.

To one who knows the right thing to do, and does not do it, to him it is sin. James 4:17.

Prayer: Thank you, Father, for making it clear through your word and your voice what you want me to obey. I confess that I often do not obey, even though I say I will. Please forgive me. Help me to follow your lead as you show me what you want me to obey. Please impress on me that actually obeying you is the only true obedience, and that through my obedience I can show how much I love you. And please, Father, draw me ever closer to you as I choose to obey, expressing my love for you. Thank you I can and do bring these prayers before you in the name of Jesus. Amen.

Think on this: All of us have purposefully disobeyed God. What do you think motivates such disobedience? What would it look like to live a life in total obedience to God? Is that possible? Why or why not? If it is possible, do you think you can do it on your own? If no, what help do you need? How can you receive that help?

DAY 23

The Basics of Discipleship: It's Optional

"Awhile back I mentioned discipleship," Stan began. "I said we'd be spending a lot of time on the subject."

"I remember," I replied. "I'm still not sure what the word means, or what being a disciple looks like."

"I think it's at the heart of being a Christian," Stan replied. "It's a big subject, with a lot of moving parts."

"Moving parts? In what way?"

"Simple example," Stan replied. "A disciple is a person. One person discipling another is a continuing process of that person coming alongside the other."

"Like walking together?"

"That's it. And it involves sharing, leading, modeling, teaching, demonstrating, and all sorts of things like that. In your Bible study, have you come across anything Jesus said about being a disciple?"

"Well, I remember that He said to deny self."

"Did you notice what He said right before that?"

"Not really," I admitted.

"Jesus began with 'If anyone wants to be a disciple.' And that 'if' is very important. Much, maybe all, of what I do as a Christian is a choice. And being a disciple certainly involves choosing to be a disciple. Discipleship doesn't just happen all by itself."

"Wouldn't it be a lot easier if it did?" I asked.

"Yes, certainly," Stan replied, "it probably would be easier, but that's not the way God set it up. I think God makes it real clear what He wants, but He doesn't force the matter. He's not going to force me to be a disciple. But he does make it real clear that, to be on the path towards maturity in my faith, choosing to be a disciple is absolutely essential."

Bible verses to consider:
If anyone wishes to come after Me, let him deny himself, and take up his cross, and follow Me. Matthew 16:24.

If anyone wishes to come after Me, let him deny himself, and take up his cross daily, and follow Me. Luke 9:23.

Prayer: Thank you, Father, for allowing me to be a disciple of your Son. Thank you, too, for making it clear to me that being a disciple is something I have to choose; that it will not happen all by itself. I confess that too often I have not chosen to be a disciple, because I did not know what it meant, and I chose to go my own way rather than yours. Forgive me, and help me follow your lead, choosing to be the disciple you intend. Thank you I can and do bring these prayers before you in the name of Jesus. Amen.

Think on this: Do you agree that being a disciple of Christ is optional? Why or why not? If you agree it is optional, how do you make the choice? Do you think a person can be a Christian without being a disciple of Christ? Why or why not? Is choosing to be a disciple a one-time choice, or is it ongoing?

DAY 24

Being Ready to Ask, "Can I Pray for You?"

One morning as we were ending our time together, Stan said, "I noticed a new bakery on my walk over here. They have some great looking pastries. Want to meet there tomorrow and give them a try?"

"Sounds good to me," I replied. "Where is it?"

"At the corner of fourth and Grove," Stan said.

"I can find that," I said. "How's seven-thirty?"

"Perfect," Stan said. "I'll be there."

Then next morning Stan was waiting for me at a table in the back. "Just got here," he said.

"Smells like something good is going on!" I replied.

The waitress came. "Can I get you some coffee while you decide what you'd like?"

"Sure thing," Stan replied.

We both decided the eclairs looked good. When the waitress returned for our order, Stan said to her, "We're going to pray and thank God for His blessing before we enjoy those goodies. Is there anything we can pray for you?"

Looking surprised, she replied, "Let me think about that."

After she left, I told Stan, "That was an amazing thing you just did. Do you do that often?"

"Only as the Spirit leads," he replied, "but I've found the more I follow, the more He leads!"

"Do you think she'll have anything for us to pray about?"

"We'll see," he answered.

When the waitress brought our eclairs she said, "I've been thinking about what you asked. How did you know I needed prayer?" Then, without waiting for Stan to answer, she said, "My younger brother is in terrible shape. He has a bad addiction to pain pills. He really needs help. Would you pray for him?"

"Sure will," Stan said. "And not that God doesn't know, but can you tell us your brother's name?"

"Jake," she said.

Stan prayed while she stood there. When he finished, she thanked him.

After she left, Stan said, "That's why we were led here today. It's going to be real interesting to see how God answers that prayer for Jake."

"Do you think we will ever know?" I asked.

"That's up to the Lord," Stan responded. "My role is to be obedient. When God brings people into my life who need prayer, I am to pray. If I don't know their need, I am to ask them. The results are up to God!"

Bible verse to consider:
First of all, then, I urge that entreaties and prayers, petitions, and thanksgivings, be made on behalf of all men. 1 Timothy 2:1.

Prayer: Thank you, Father, for allowing me to come before you in prayer. Thank you for allowing me to pray for what is on my mind and heart. I confess that too often I do not pray for others, or even ask about their needs and struggles. Please forgive my self-centeredness. Help me follow your lead and to pay attention to the needs of others. Give me boldness and discernment when I offer to pray, whether for friends or strangers. Thank you that no one is a stranger to you. Thank you I can and do bring these, and all prayers, before you in the name of Jesus. Amen.

Think on this: Asking others, especially strangers, if you can pray for them is not easy. Have you ever done that? If so, what happened? If you have not, why? Do you think the more you try, the easier it will become? How do you feel when someone asks to pray for your needs?

DAY 25

Not Maintaining a Separate Identity

"I'm not sure I've mentioned this before," said Stan, "but I've noticed that the apostle Paul often uses one very small word to say something very important."

"You have an example?" I asked.

"Sure do," Stan replied. "I'm thinking of the word '*in*.' Especially in his letter to the Colossian church—which is also a letter to you and me, don't forget!"

"How can one little word matter so much?" I asked.

"It matters, because Paul was stating a significant truth about our life as believers in Jesus Christ. He wrote that we need to 'walk in Him.' He didn't say 'with.' In fact, again and again Paul writes about how we are 'in Christ.'"

"What's so significant about 'in' versus 'with'?" I asked. "Seems like a small difference."

"It may seem so," Stan said, "but I think Paul is making a vital distinction. If I'm walking 'with' Christ, it's kind of like I'm doing so as an individual apart from Him."

"You mean maintaining an identity separate from Him?" I asked.

"That seems like a good way to put it," Stan replied. "But if I'm walking 'in' Christ, I exist as a person united with Him."

"That sounds about like how God describes marriage," I replied, "where He says that the two shall become one."

"Exactly, my friend," Stan responded. "I believe that once I became a Christian, my faith walk is to be 'in' Jesus, not just 'with' Him. I am no longer who I was, and I won't want to be. I no longer want an identity apart from Him."

"How do I keep aware of my new identity?" I asked.

"Choose," he said simply.

"I'm thinking of an earlier conversation we had," I said. "Does this include choosing to ask the Holy Spirit to change me?"

"Yes," he said. "I have to get myself out of the way, choose to be who God wants me be, choose to do what He wants me to do, and choose to follow wherever He wants me to go."

"Sounds like being a disciple," I said.

"You've got it, my friend," Stan replied. "And as I chose those things, my faith walk will be <u>in</u> Christ, not just <u>with</u> Him while maintaining a separate identity."

Bible verses to consider:
As you therefore have received Christ Jesus the Lord, so walk in Him. Colossians 2:6.

Or do you not know that your body is a temple of the Holy Spirit who is in you, whom you have from God, and that you are not your own? For you have been bought with a price; therefore glorify God in your body. 1 Corinthians 6:19-20.

For this cause a man shall leave his father and his mother, and shall cleave to his wife; and they shall become one flesh. Genesis 2:24.

Prayer: Thank you, Father, for your provision that I can walk in Christ, not just with Him. I confess that too often I want to maintain my separate identity as I walk with Him. Please forgive me. And please lead me, and help me to follow, so that I truly become one with Jesus in everything. Help me take deeply to heart the truth that I am no longer my own, because Jesus redeemed me on the cross. Thank you I can and do bring these prayers before you in His name. Amen.

Think on this: Do you agree with the difference between walking "in" Christ versus walking "with" Him? Why or why not? How would you describe your faith walk? Is it as deep and as consistent as you would like? If no, what would it take for you to have a deeper and more consistent walk? Is that something you would like? If so, are you willing to do what can make it happen? Why or why not?

DAY 26

The Parking Space Wasn't that Important

As I joined Stan at our table one morning, I noticed he looked a bit downcast. "Anything bothering you?" I asked.

"You're too observant," he responded with a slight smile.

"Anything you want to talk about?" I asked.

"Promise you won't think less or me?"

"Promise," I said.

"Well, I blew it again yesterday afternoon," he began.

"What was going on?" I asked.

"My wife and I went out to do some shopping, which we always enjoy. We were going to have lunch at Carole's Cafe and then go to one of our favorite stores to see about gift ideas for the holidays. Both of us were looking forward to a nice time, but I ruined it before we even got started."

"What happened?" I asked.

"I happened," Stan said. "I let my ugly old self rise up and get angry about someone taking 'my' parking place. Rather than just let it go, I really lost my cool. I said some ugly things, and it made me realize I'm not where I like to think I am in my relationship with God. I sure didn't do a very good job manifesting Him. I clearly manifested the exact opposite of who I claim to be as a Christian."

"Sorry to hear that," I replied.

"You're not the only one!" he said.

Continuing, he said, "Do you know what it means to close someone's spirit?"

Before I could answer, he went on, with obvious frustration. "What I said and how I acted closed my wife's spirit so much that I had, in a thoughtless instant, ruined what could have been a very nice outing. After my outburst, my wife said she had lost her enthusiasm for doing anything with me. We went home, and I spent a frosty afternoon and evening." Then more to himself than to me, he said, "Will I ever learn? I've read in Proverbs countless times about a hot-tempered man stirring up strife, but only when I do the stirring do I really see the truth of that wisdom."

With a verbal jab, I said, "Is it fair to say the parking spot probably wasn't as important as you thought it was?"

"Amen," he responded. "Amen!"

Bible verses to consider:
A hot-tempered man stirs up strife, but the slow to anger pacifies contention. Proverbs 15:18.

A perverse man spreads strife, and a slanderer separates intimate friends. Proverbs 16:28.

If any man is in Christ, he is a new creature; the old things passed away; behold new things have come. 2 Corinthians 5:17.

Prayer: Thank you, Father, I can come before you in confession and repentance, knowing you hear and respond out of your love, grace, and mercy. I confess that way too often I do not manifest you by my thoughts, words, and actions. I choose to manifest the old self, rather than the new creation as you intend. Please forgive me. And please help me get the old me out of your way, so you can manifest your whole self in and through me. I pray for the fruit of your Spirit to be shown, rather than the fruit of self, the world, the flesh, and the devil. Thank you I can and do bring these prayers before you in the name of your Son, whose Spirit is in me to be manifested. Amen.

Think on this: Just when we think the old self is under control, we do and say things that clearly show that's not the case. Have you ever experienced that? Do you think there is a solution? If no, why not? If yes, what would it look like to pursue the solution? What part does confession and repentance play? How about denial of self?

DAY 27

Ready to be Taught?

"My wife and I had dinner last night at the Good Fortune Chinese Restaurant," said Stan.

"Nice time?" I asked.

"Great," he said. "The service is terrific, the food is always good, and they usually have great fortune cookies!"

"Did you get a good one last night?"

"Sometimes I think there's someone in the back room writing fortunes just for me," he laughed.

"Last night, mine had a special meaning to me."

"What did it say?"

"'When the student is ready, the teacher will come.' I know it's just a fortune in a cookie, but it really does contain a significant truth for my faith walk with God."

"How so?" I asked.

"Well, when God awakened in me the desire to know Him, I responded by drawing near to Him. As we've discussed before, when I chose to draw near to God, He responded by drawing near to me. That first step was just the beginning."

"The beginning of what?" I asked.

"The process of knowing God," Stan replied. "And knowing God the Father and Jesus the Son is how Jesus defined eternal life. I was ready for the lessons to begin, and God began to teach me. And as I'm continually open to being taught what He has for me, He fills me–and keeps on filling me–with the knowledge of Himself."

"And where does that filling come from?" I asked.

"First," Stan replied, "it comes through God's written word, the Bible. It also comes through the voice of the indwelling Holy Spirit, as well as through people God brings into my life for His purposes. But I must stay open and ready to be taught."

"And conversely," I ventured, "if a person is not ready, they won't be capable of learning."

"Exactly," Stan agreed. "I have to be ready, and I have to be teachable. It's just like any other subject. Picture this: a student is sitting in class with headphones on, blasting music into his ears. You think he's ready to hear the voice of the teacher?"

"Not so much," I replied.

"I may not be wearing headphones," Stan said, "but my own worries, selfish desires, or the devil's temptations can seem to drown out the voice of the Spirit. When that happens, do you think I'm set to learn what God has for me?"

"Same answer," I replied. "Not so much!"

Bible verses to consider:
So that your trust may be in the Lord, I have taught you today, even you. Proverbs 22:19.

Draw near to God and He will draw near to you. James 4:8.

And this is eternal life that they may know Thee, the only true God, and Jesus Christ whom Thou hast sent. John 17:3.

Prayer: Thank you, Father, for wanting me to know you. Thank you for being willing to teach me so I will know you. I confess that too often I am not teachable, because I'm not ready to be taught. Please forgive me, and give me a more teachable spirit so that I can have a deeper knowledge of you. Open me to want to want be taught by your Spirit and from your word. Please fill me and keep on filling me with the knowledge of you. Thank you I can and do bring these prayers before you in the name of Jesus. Amen.

Think on this: Do you think it is important to know God ever more deeply? Are you satisfied with your present knowledge of God? Why or why not? Do you think you have a teachable spirit? Explain. If you sense you are not as teachable as God may want, have you asked for His help?

DAY 28

Why Do You Refuse the Help?

Ricky had just filled our coffee cups. I took a sip, but the coffee was much hotter than I expected. I jerked the cup away, spilling half of it on the table.

As I grabbed napkins to clean up, Stan did the same, saying, "Let me help you."

"No, I've got it," I said sharply, out of embarrassment.

So Stan put down his napkins and let me clean up the mess. When the table was dry again, and Ricky had refilled my cup, Stan said, "What just happened here?"

"I spilled my coffee," I said rather defensively.

"What else?"

"I cleaned it up," I answered.

"Anything else?" Stan asked.

Knowing he had a lesson in mind, I said, "You tell me."

"I offered my help, and you refused that offer," Stan said.

"Did I offend you with that?"

"No," Stan replied, "but I think there's a lesson here. A lesson I keep trying to learn myself."

"What's that?" I asked.

"I have in me the Holy Spirit," Stan responded. "You have the same Holy Spirit, as does every believer. Jesus called Him the Helper. I am in constant need of His help—and He is always there to offer it. But way too often, my response is like yours just now: I say, 'No, I've got it.' I rely on myself and my own abilities, rather than relying on the Helper sent from God."

"What if I refuse to accept His help?" I asked. "Will He leave me in my mess?"

"He is faithful," Stan said, "and promises never to forsake us. But when we actively ask for His help, we are growing in our relationship with Him, and we can recognize His work in our life. You might say He's capable of cleaning up a whole lot better than we can on our own!"

Bible verses to consider:
But I tell you the truth, it is to your advantage that I go away; for if I do not go away, the Helper will not come to you; but if I go, I will send Him to you. John 16:7.

And do not grieve the Holy Spirit of God, by whom you were sealed for the day of redemption. Ephesians 4:30.

Apart from Me you can do nothing. John 15:5.

Prayer: Thank you, Father, for all the help you provide, in every aspect of my life. You know how terribly self-focused I am, and how I think I can do things on my own. Please forgive all that foolishness. Help my first response, in any situation, be to seek the help of the Holy Spirit. I am grateful that His help is always available. Thank you I can and do bring these prayers before you in the name of Jesus. Amen.

Think on this: We all allow our self-sufficiency or self-focus to get in the way of what God wants to do for us. Why do you think we purposefully refuse God's help? Why is the Holy Spirit called the Helper? What is it He wants to help us with? If you sense you are not getting the help that He offers, would you like to change that? If so, do you know how?

DAY 29

The Importance of the Check-Up

"I had to schedule my annual physical yesterday," Stan began, "and it occurred to me that check-ups are important for all kinds of health."

"How many kinds are there?" I asked.

"Well, of course there's physical health. There's mental health, emotional health, and the health of my relationships. There's also financial health, the health of my legal matters, and general societal health. Plus a whole lot more. But one is absolutely essential to me."

"What's that?" I asked.

"Spiritual health. I mean the health of my faith walk and relationship with God," Stan replied.

"Is there a checkup for that?" I asked.

"Definitely," he said. "I've found that an essential part of reading the Bible is looking for verses that offer questions. By answering those questions for myself, I can 'check-up' where I am in my faith walk."

"I know my doctor always has questions prepared. Are you saying God's word does, too?"

"Yes," Stan said. "Let's say I'm proceeding in my faith walk in a way that I think is right, without regularly checking with God to see if it's right in His sight. There's always the chance I've headed off in the wrong direction."

"And you think there are Bible verses that help you with that?" I asked.

"Absolutely," Stan responded. "For example, John in his gospel relates a discussion between Jesus and his disciple Philip. What they talked about nails this for me. Jesus asked Philip a question that's essential to ask myself regularly."

"What is it?"

"In essence, Jesus asked, 'Have we been together this long, and you still don't know Me?'"

"Wow!" I replied, "that's a powerful question for anyone to ask another person. But it's really powerful when you consider it's coming from the Son of God."

"You've got that right, my friend," Stan said. "And that's why I call it a 'check-up' verse. Am I proceeding down the path of knowing God more deeply? Or have I been spending my time as a Christian without growing in my knowledge of God? It's essential to remember that Jesus defined eternal life as knowing God the Father and Jesus the Son. That's what I am to pursue while I remain on this side of eternity."

"Before boarding the train for eternity in God's presence," I added.

"Exactly," he said. "When I seriously consider the questions God poses in His word, I'm allowing the Holy Spirit to ask how deeply I know the Father and the Son. And I have to be ready to answer in all honesty. That's the way to get a diagnosis about my spiritual health."

"And then make whatever adjustments are necessary?" I replied.

"That's right," said Stan.

I thought for a moment, then said, "That sounds to me like confession and repentance."

"And that's another great conversation for another day!" said Stan.

Bible verses to consider:
Jesus said to him, "Have I been so long with you, and yet you have not come to know Me, Philip?" John 14:9.

Every man's way is right in his own eyes, but the Lord weighs the hearts. Proverbs 21:2.

And this is eternal life, that they may know Thee, the only true God, and Jesus Christ whom Thou hast sent. John 17:3.

Prayer: Thank you, Father, for providing the way for me to spend eternity with you when it is time. Thank you, too, that I can pursue knowing you and your Son on this side of eternity. Thank you for providing questions in your word that help me know you better and discover areas where I need to change. I confess that too often I have chosen not to read your word or listen to your voice. Please forgive and help me follow every step of your lead into an ever-deepening, ever-growing, personal relationship just as you intend. Thank you I can and do bring these prayers before you in the name of Jesus. Amen.

Think on this: Do you think it is possible to know God? Why or why not? How would you answer the "check-up" question that Jesus asked Philip? Are you willing to have God, through the Holy Spirit, ask you about knowing Him? What does it look like to pursue knowing God as deeply as possible? There are "check-up verses" throughout the Bible if we have our eyes open to see them. Have you discovered any that are helpful to you, which may be helpful to others?

DAY 30

Being Used to Answer Prayers

"Have you ever been used by God to answer another person's prayer?" Stan asked one morning.

"I don't know," I replied. "I'm not sure I've ever thought about that. Have you?"

"Yes," he said, "God has used me that way. I think that is part of being one of God's children. He uses us to bless others."

"Bless others? How does that fit in?"

"Jesus spoke of doing good works so that others might glorify God. I believe I am to bless others in His name and for His sake, so that they will have their vision of God expanded and enhanced. Then they, in turn, will go on to glorify God."

"What kind of blessing are you talking about?" I asked. "Money?"

"Blessings can be financial. But they can also be far more valuable than money," Stan replied.

"For example, blessing another person with the truth of the gospel is precious and priceless."

"Priceless?" I asked.

"Yes, because God's truth can change people forever. It can change their eternal destination, as well as how they live on this side of eternity. Those people can then, in their own way, become a blessing to others. And on and on it goes," he added. "That's how the church is built, and that's how it grows."

"I'd love to hear an example of how God has used you that way," I said.

"Sure," Stan replied. "Here's a simple example. Recently I was part of a prayer group that met after the Sunday service. One of the women in the group asked for prayer for her husband. He needed a new job, because his employer was going out of business."

"How did that involve you?"

"In a remarkable way. Just the day before, one of my neighbors had mentioned to me that his employer was hiring. I was able to tell the woman. Her husband applied, and now has a new job."

"So," I said, "because you heard a prayer request, you were able to be a part of God's answer."

"Exactly," Stan said. "And that's why I want to always be available for what God wants to do in and through me."

"What about a situation where a person may pray, but you are nowhere near enough to hear the prayer? How can God use you in that situation?" I asked.

"Give me an example," Stan replied.

"Say there's a person on the corner asking for money," I said. "Say, further, that he's been praying to God for someone to help him. You come by. What then?"

"That happens all the time," Stan replied. "And every time it does, I ask the Holy Spirit to lead me. I ask whether or not He intends for me to help."

"Do you always get the same answer?" I asked.

"I do not," Stan said. "Sometimes I'm prompted to help, and I obey, giving the person something in the name of Jesus. Other times I'm not prompted in the same way. But the essential part," he concluded, "is being alert to opportunities God puts before me, to be part of His answer to the prayers of others. If I'm alert and I obey, I know God is pleased."

Bible verses to consider:
Let your light shine before men in such a way that they may see your good works and glorify your Father who is in heaven. Matthew 5:16.

If you love Me, you will keep my commandments. John 14:15.

Prayer: Thank you, Father, for answering prayers. Thank you for allowing me to be part of your answers to the prayers of others. I confess that too often I do not pay sufficient attention to the prayers and needs of others, because of my self-focus. Forgive me and help me stay available to be used by you. Thank you I can and do bring these prayers before you in the name of Jesus. Amen.

Think on this: Being used by God to help answer the prayers of others is a great privilege. Have you experienced being used in that way? If so, what was it like? Have you ever missed an opportunity to be used? Were you able to do anything about the missed opportunity? How can you be open to how God wants to use you? Has anyone ever told you that you were an answer to their prayers? How did that encourage you in your faith walk?

DAY 31

Set Apart to Be a Part

"Sanctification," Stan said one morning, "is a big word for a big subject. Most everything we talk about relates to it in one way or another."

"Can you give me a sketch of what sanctification looks like?" I asked.

"Well," he replied, "I think it's not so much what it looks like, but rather what I look like."

"What you look like? What's that mean?"

"It seems to me," said Stan, "that sanctification is basically setting something apart for its intended purpose. If you're talking about a Christian being sanctified, it's about that person being set apart for God's intended purpose."

"Set apart from what?"

"From everything contrary to God," Stan replied, "as well as apart from my old life, when I was more 'set apart' for myself, doing what I wanted apart from God."

"Is sanctification up to the individual person?" I asked.

"'On the one hand, no. But on the other, yes."

"How can it be both 'no' and 'yes'?"

"The 'no' part," said Stan, "is that sanctification is God's work. Just as I could not save myself, I cannot sanctify myself."

"How about the yes part?"

"I think desiring to be sanctified is something I can experience. I make the choices, while God is always supplying the power and grace. As Paul put it, 'God is at work in you' to give both the desire *and* the ability to do His work. It's like we talked about with discipleship. God wants me to be a disciple, and I must make the choices to follow Him. But in the end, He gets all the glory."

"Okay," I replied, "if I have the desire for God do what He wants in and through me, what happens next?"

"You continue moving down the path of transformation, that began with your conversion and leads toward spiritual maturity."

"And when does it end?" I asked.

"It's a life-long journey," Stan said, "regardless of how long that life may be. I believe God intends for me to walk that path as long as He keeps me on this side of eternity. If I ever stop, I will have either boarded the train to glory, or I will have started down a wrong path, heading in a wrong direction. I will no longer be a part of why God has set me apart."

"Be a part of why God has set me apart," I repeated. "I think I can remember that!"

Bibles verses to consider:
For it is God who is at work in you, both to will and to work for His good pleasure. Philippians 2:13.

Sanctify them in your truth. John 17:17.

Therefore if any man is in Christ, he is a new creature; the old things passed away; behold new things have come. 2 Corinthians 5:17.

Prayer: Thank you, Father, for giving me the assurance of spending eternity with you when it's time. Thank you, too, for leaving me on this side of eternity so I can pursue knowing you. Thank you that this involves choosing to walk the path of transformation from conversion towards spiritual maturity. Thank you for wanting to use me for your purposes, setting me apart for you. I confess that too often I choose to be set apart for me, the world, the flesh, and the devil, rather than set apart for you. Please forgive me. Help me follow every step of your lead so that I choose to allow you to sanctify me in accordance with your will. Thank you I can and do bring these prayers before you in the name of Jesus. Amen.

Think on this: What does being "set apart" for God look like to you? Is it a one-time decision or a way of life? Where are you on the path of being set apart for God? If you do not sense you are being set apart for God's intended purposes, what's missing? Who can supply what may be missing? What would it look like to be fully committed to allowing God to do His sanctifying work in and through you? Is that what you want? Why or why not?

DAY 32

Working it Out

"I had an interesting conversation with a neighbor last night," Stan began.

"About what?" I asked.

"Working out his salvation," Stan replied.

"Working his way to heaven?" I asked.

"No," Stan said, "he is secure in the knowledge of his salvation as a free and gracious gift from God. He knows he can't work his way to heaven. But he didn't seem to know he was supposed to do something with the gift he's been given."

"Do something?" I repeated. "Like what?"

"Do you remember what the stationmaster told you at the beginning of your faith walk? We are to be something we've never been and do things we've never done. This being and doing is at the heart of working out the salvation that has been worked in."

"I'm still not sure what 'working out' means," I said.

"In light of all that God has graciously done for me," Stan replied, "I respond in gratitude. I am to honor him in every area of my life for as long as He keeps me here."

"And your neighbor didn't know that?" I asked.

"I don't think he wanted to know," Stan said.

"Didn't want to know? How so?"

"This neighbor is fond of saying, 'Don't bother me, I'm retired.' He says it in jest, meaning he wants to enjoy resting in retirement. But I think he sees his Christianity in kind of the same light."

"How so?" I asked.

"It's as if he says to God, 'Don't bother me. I've got my ticket to glory.'"

"What do you think God might say back to him?"

"I believe God would say, 'I gave you that ticket. Now live a life that shows your gratitude, and shows the world who I am.'"

"So," I said, "do you think your conversation with your neighbor is going to make a difference?"

"That's my prayer," Stan replied. "I believe if we all made a bigger effort to work out what God has worked in, the church and the world would be a much finer place."

Bible verses to consider:
They will still yield fruit in advanced age; they will be full of sap and very green, to declare that the LORD is just; He is my rock, and there is no malice in Him. Psalm 92:14-15.

Work out your salvation with fear and trembling; for it is God who is at work in you, both to will and to work for His good pleasure. Philippians 2:12-13.

Or do you not know that your body is the temple of the Holy Spirit who is in you, whom you have from God, and that you are not your own? For you have been bought with a price: therefore glorify God in your body. 1 Corinthians 6:19-20.

Everyone who is proud in heart is an abomination to the Lord. Proverbs 16:5.

Prayer: Father, thank you for the assurance of salvation resulting from the life, death, and resurrection of Jesus. Thank you for those who brought the truth of salvation to me. Please keep me from falling into the trap of thinking that assurance of salvation is the end of my story. Help me to work out my salvation by living a life of gratitude for your grace. Forgive me for the times I want to retire from serving you. Give me strength to serve you all my days. Thank you I can and do bring these prayers before you in the name of Jesus. Amen.

Think on this: Do you agree that you are to work out the salvation that has been worked in? Why or why not? Are there areas in your life where you have "retired" too soon? Do you think there is a connection between pursuing discipleship and working out your salvation? If so, how would you describe that connection?

DAY 33

Is there an Escape?

"Stan," I began one morning, "do you ever find yourself falling into the same old sins that lead you away from God?"

"You might as well ask if I ever find myself breathing!" said Stan. "Thankfully, God is gracious. He knows I am weak when faced with temptation. It's part of life on this side of glory. But I've found a way to use my weakness to strengthen my faith walk."

"Using weakness for strength?" I said.

"Exactly!" Stan replied. "The apostle Paul wrote to the Corinthians that God won't allow me to be tempted beyond what I can handle."

"How does a person 'handle' temptation?"

"First, I have to admit my weakness. Then I ask God for His strength to overcome whatever temptation I'm facing. Paul says, 'God is faithful,' so I know He sees my struggle and He wants to help."

"What exactly causes the struggle?" I asked.

"Same old stuff," Stan replied. "Self, the world, the flesh, and the devil. Don't forget that Satan just loves to get Christians thinking they can do nothing about temptation. He wants us to focus on our failures instead of God's faithfulness. But God wants to direct our focus to the cross, where Jesus took the punishment for all our sins. And then He wants us to pray when tempted. He has all the power and strength we need. Paul calls it 'providing the way of escape.'"

"Escape from temptation sure sounds good," I replied. "Why wouldn't people ask for that help?"

"I think you know the answer to that," Stan replied.

"Focusing on self, rather than on God," I responded. "Focusing on what I want to do apart from God, rather than on what God wants. Following what I want to follow apart from God, rather than following His lead."

"You got it, my friend," Stan replied.

Bible verses to consider:
No temptation has overtaken you but such as is common to man; and God is faithful, who will not allow you to be tempted beyond what you are able, but with the temptation will provide the way of escape also, so that you will be able to endure it. 1 Corinthians 10:13.

God is faithful, through whom you were called into fellowship with His Son, Jesus Christ, our Lord. 1 Corinthians 1:9.

The Lord knows how to rescue the godly from temptation…." 2 Peter 2:9.

Prayer: Thank you, Father, for all your love, grace, and mercy. Thank you for your strength that can overcome my weaknesses. I acknowledge my weakness and confess that too often I take my sins as a fact, rather than seeking your strength to overcome them. I know that when I do that, I am pleasing Satan rather than you. Please forgive that foolishness. And please, Father, help me follow every step of your lead so I will claim your strength to overcome the weaknesses I face in my life. Thank you I can and do bring these prayers before you in the name of Jesus. Amen.

Think on this: We all face temptation. Those temptations can be overcome by God's strength. Do you believe that? Why or why not? Do you have weaknesses that need to be overcome by God's strength? What "way of escape" do you think He might provide? Have you experienced God's faithfulness when you've been tempted?

DAY 34

He Sees the Whole Picture

"I'm not what you'd call a big fan of country music," Stan said one morning, "but some of the songs sure do have a great message."

"Anything particular in mind?" I asked.

"Yes," he replied. "Garth Brooks has one that's really instructive for me. It's about being thankful for unanswered prayer."

"Unanswered?" I replied. "I thought God answers all prayers, but sometimes with 'No' or 'Wait' or something else."

"Well," Stan said, "I think you're right, but that would have made Mr. Brook's lyrics a whole lot more complicated! In any event, I think the song is an accurate reflection of praying for things and being thankful God didn't answer the way the person wanted."

"How so?" I replied. "How could a person be thankful for that?"

"Seeing in retrospect that he prayed for the wrong thing," Stan replied. "Or seeing that his request was for something less than the best from God's storehouse."

"Have you had that experience?"

"For sure. Shortly after I became a Christian, I was in a situation where I really wanted to change jobs. I was unsettled where I was and thought it was time to move on. There was an opening for a job I really wanted. I applied for it. I prayed and prayed, telling God how much I wanted the job. But it was offered to someone else."

"That must have been a disappointment for you," I said. "Were you mad at God?"

"I was really disappointed, but, no, I can't say I was mad at God. And when I realized He had a different plan for me–one that was much better than my own–I was very thankful He hadn't given me what I prayed for. If I had been offered that job, I wouldn't have seen God use me in my original job."

"How did He use you?" I asked.

"In many ways, but those are stories for other days," Stan replied. "For now, just remember the bottom line: that God knows what you need more than you do. And He loves you too much not to give you His best. That will keep you from wallowing in disappointment when you don't get 'your' answer."

"Can't people avoid the disappointment by praying in accordance with God's will in the first place?"

"You're right," Stan replied, "but that's not as easy as it sounds. I think there are three things to keep in mind."

"What three things?"

"First, I pray as best as I know how. Second, I trust the Holy Spirit to intercede as He knows best. Third, I know that God sees the whole picture, and I don't. Whatever way He answers, it will always be for my good and His glory."

"You know, Stan," I said, "I can see why you said this might complicate the lyrics to that song!"

Bible verses to consider:

Seek first His kingdom and His righteousness, and all these things shall be added to you. Matthew 6:33.

Father, if Thou art willing, remove this cup from Me; yet not My will, but Thine be done. Luke 22:42.

And in the same way the Spirit also helps our weakness; for we do not know how to pray as we should, but the Spirit Himself intercedes for us with groanings too deep for words; and He who searches the hearts knows what the mind of the Spirit is, because He intercedes for the saints according to the will of God. Romans 8:26-27.

Prayer: Thank you, Father, that you allow me to come before you in prayer, in the name of your Son. Thank you that you hear and answer all my prayers. Thank you, too, that the Holy Spirit intercedes for me. Help me follow every step of your lead, to pray in accordance with your will. I ask you to teach me, beyond a shadow of doubt, that your answers are always best, even though I may be disappointed for the moment. Thank you I can and do bring these prayers before you in the name of Jesus. Amen.

Think on this: Do you believe that God answers all prayers? Why or why not? Have you ever been in a situation where you were thankful that God did not answer your prayers in the way you prayed? If so, what did you learn from that experience? Have you ever been in a situation where you simply did not know how to pray? If so, what did that feel like? What did you do?

DAY 35

How Are You Doing?

“Morning, Stan,” I said as I joined him at the table. “How are you doing today?”

To my surprise, instead of his usual ‘Fine, thanks,’ he said, “Great question!”

“I didn’t intend it to be a great question,” I said, a bit defensively. “I was just greeting you.”

“I know,” Stan replied, “but your question raises an important point.”

“In what way?” I asked.

“‘How am I doing?’ is a question God wants me to think about.”

“How you’re doing about what?”

“My relationship with Him. How am I doing? Am I growing? Am I becoming more spiritually mature? Am I making progress on the road from conversion to transformation?”

“What about ‘how am I doing’ regarding being in God’s eternal presence?”

“That’s a whole different question,” Stan replied, “with a Yes or No answer about life eternally with God when it’s time. Either I have my ticket for the train to glory, or I don’t.”

“Okay, got it,” I said. “No working your way to heaven.”

“Exactly,” Stan responded. “What I’m talking about is life here and now. Am I living as the person God intends me to be? Am I serving in ways He has planned for me? I think it’s essential for my relationship with God to ask Him, ‘How am I doing?’”

“How do you do that?” I asked.

"I start by praying about it," Stan replied. "And I can tell you this: when I'm open to asking God, and open to hearing and listening to His response, I have a great sense of His love, kindness, and compassion towards me. God wants an ever-growing, ever-deepening relationship with me. He does not force it, but when I ask Him, 'How I am doing?' He is eager to reassure me of His love and help as I follow His lead. It's a great feeling!"

"Since it's so great," I said with a smile, "why don't you ask Him more often?"

Stan paused, and then said, "Another great question!"

Bible verses to consider:
I [Paul]…entreat you to walk in a manner worthy of the calling with which you have been called. Ephesians 4:1.

For this reason we also, since the day we heard, have not ceased praying for you and asking that you may be filled with the knowledge of His will in all spiritual wisdom and understanding, so that you will walk in a manner worthy of the Lord, to please Him in all respects, bearing fruit in every good work and increasing in the knowledge of God. Colossians 1:9-10

And Jesus kept increasing in wisdom and stature, and in favor with God and men. Luke 2:24.

Prayer: Thank you, Father, for wanting me to have an ever-deepening relationship with you. Thank you for faithfully moving me along the path of transformation toward greater spiritual maturity. I confess I often do not use the means you have available for me to pursue knowing you. It is my foolish choice to do what I want apart from you. Please remind me to ask you more often how I am doing, and help me follow every step of your lead, being totally open to hearing your response. Thank you I can and do bring these prayers before you in the name of Jesus. Amen.

Think on this: Do you think it is important to ask God, "How am I doing?" Do you think God wants you to ask that question? Is asking and listening for His answer a necessary part of recognizing the need for changes in your relationship with Him? Do you see asking the question as an integral part of confession and repentance? Why or why not?

DAY 36

The Importance of Listening, Not Just Hearing

"I've been making my way through Mark's gospel," Stan said. "I got to chapter eight this morning: the story of the transfiguration. Jesus went to a mountain with the disciples Peter, James, and John."

"I remember that story a bit," I replied. "Isn't it called the transfiguration because Jesus was changed in appearance?"

"That's right."

"And as I recall, Elijah and Moses showed up, and they were talking with Jesus."

"Good memory. And as a side note, that's where and when Moses finally made it into the Promised Land. But at the time, those three disciples had no idea what to make of the whole scene. In fact, Mark says they were 'terrified.' And I can well imagine it! They were seeing things they had never seen before. They somehow recognized Moses and Elijah, but what God wanted them to recognize about Jesus was the key point."

"Didn't God speak to them from a cloud?"

"Yes. Can you imagine that? The Lord God Almighty spoke out loud to the disciples. He told them what they were supposed to do with Jesus: 'Listen!' And that is what the Holy Spirit continues to tell you and me. He doesn't say 'hear,' He says 'Listen'."

"Isn't that just a distinction without a difference?" I asked. "Hearing versus listening?"

"I don't think so," Stan replied. "I think there's an important difference. If you doubt that," he added with a smile, "just ask my wife!"

"I remember the story about your friend's Hawaiian vacation," I laughed. "His wife sure caught him not listening!"

"Certainly a key way to show love to our wives, or anyone close to us, is giving them our full attention when they speak," said Stan. "And how much more we need to give Jesus our full attention when He speaks! He's the greatest authority, after all—Peter, James and John sure found that out in a big way, there on the mountain! By choosing to listen to what Jesus says, it's like I'm taking ownership of it. I am, in essence, making it my own. And then comes the obedience part."

Bible verses to consider:
Then a cloud formed, overshadowing them, and a voice came out of the cloud, "This is My beloved Son, listen to Him!" Mark 9:7.

And we ourselves heard this utterance made from heaven when we were with Him on the holy mountain. 1 Peter 1:17.

Prayer: Thank you, Father, for wanting me to listen to your Son. Thank you that His disciples heard and saw Him in person, and you inspired them to write down His words. Thank you that He still speaks to me through His word, and that the Holy Spirit helps me listen. You know how easily I am distracted. Please forgive me and help me listen, receive, embrace, and obey all you have for me. Thank you I can and do bring these prayers before you in the name of Jesus. Amen.

Think on this: What does it mean to listen to Jesus now that we cannot physically see Him? Do you consider Him the final authority in your life? Can you say that you listen for what He has for you to be and to do? How is your life different when you do listen to Him? Have you ever examined your life to see if someone or something has greater authority to you?

DAY 37

God's Activity: Looking Back

As we were watching Ricky bounce from table to table, taking orders and bringing pancakes, Stan said, "We should talk about God's activity."

"What kind of activity are you thinking about?" I asked.

"His active work in and through me," he said. "It seems there are two directions I need to look."

"What two?" I asked.

"I think I need to be looking backwards and looking at the present."

"What about the future?" I asked.

"That's not within my ability to see," Stan said.

"But the other two are?".

"Absolutely. And having a right view of both the past and present are essential. For now, let's just examine the essential process of looking back."

"Whatever you want," I replied.

"I think," Stan said, "if I'm not regularly examining what God has already done in and through me, I will miss the opportunity to know Him better. And remember, Jesus said eternal life is about knowing Him and God the Father."

"Yes," I replied, "John 17:3!"

"You got it!" Stan said. "By examining all that has happened in my past, I can see God's goodness and greatness, and I'm able to acknowledge His loving and caring provision."

"In all things?" I asked. "I can understand wanting to recall the good things, but what about the things that aren't so good?"

"I can still testify that God has done marvelous things in and through me. Before I knew Him, I might have called some circumstances only 'bad.' But God has taught me that nothing He does in accordance with His will is bad. It's all good. I just need to see from His perspective, not from my limited, self-focused one."

"How do you do that?" I asked.

"I give it all to the Holy Spirit, asking for His help," Stan replied. "He knows, and He's ready, willing, and able to teach me all that God has for me to learn from the past. This prepares me to trust Him more. It's all through the amazing love, grace, and mercy of God."

"And so," I said, "when I remember what God has done in my past, I'm drawn into a deeper relationship with Him. Is that right?"

"Deeper and full of more gratitude," Stan said. "And that is a very good thing!"

Bible verse to consider:

We know that God causes all things to work together for good to those who love God, to those who are called according to His purpose. Romans 8:28.

Prayer: Thank you, Father, for working in and through me in the past. I confess I often don't examine with enough care what you have already done, and why you did it. Please forgive me for not taking the time to remember and review. Open my eyes to see your activity in and through my life, so that I will use those opportunities to know you better. Thank you I can and do bring these prayers before you in the name of Jesus. Amen.

Think on this: Do you believe what Romans 8:28 promises? Or does it seem like wishful thinking? How does Paul describe the believer in this verse? What do you think it means to love God? To be called according to His purpose? How can loving God and knowing you are called give you assurance that all things work together for good? What will it look like for you to have that assurance?

DAY 38

Impaired Vision?

"The other day," Stan began, "we talked a bit about the transfiguration in Mark's gospel."

"We did," I responded. "We were talking about the importance of listening to Jesus."

"Exactly. There's another part of the account I want to mention."

"What's that?" I asked.

"God the Father spoke from the cloud affirming Jesus. He called Jesus his beloved Son and said, 'Listen to Him!' Then there was no more voice, and when the cloud cleared, Moses and Elijah were gone."

"I remember," I said. "Then Jesus, Peter, James, and John, went back down the mountain."

"Right," Stan replied, "but Mark gives another detail, and it's crucial for me to remember in my faith walk with God."

"What detail?"

"Mark says the disciples looked around and saw only Jesus."

"So?" I replied.

"That's how I want to live my life on this side of eternity. When I look around, I want to see Jesus. I want every aspect of my being to be focused on Him. If I don't see Jesus where I'm looking, I'm likely focusing on my own efforts, and it's a fair guess I'm not giving Him His rightful place. There's so much to look at in the world, I can get easily distracted from what's important: Jesus' work on my behalf. I want to see Him wherever I look."

"And as you always remind me," I said, "with the help of the Holy Spirit, God leads me to where He wants me to be, looking at what He intends."

Bible verses to consider:
They looked around and saw no one with them anymore, except Jesus alone. Mark 9:8

Therefore, since we have so great a cloud of witnesses surrounding us, let us also lay aside every encumbrance and the sin which so easily entangles us, and let us run with endurance the race that is set before us, fixing our eyes on Jesus, the author and perfecter of faith, who for the joy set before Him endured the cross, despising the shame, and has sat down at the right hand of the throne of God. Hebrews 12:1-2.

Prayer: Thank you, Father, for wanting me to listen to the voice of your Son. Thank you also for wanting me to have Jesus as my chief focus. I confess I am too easily distracted by things of this world that satisfy the flesh and please the enemy. I admit that I purposefully choose to see things other than Jesus. Please focus my vision on what you intend, and not on what is unimportant from your perspective. Thank you that you do want to correct my impaired spiritual vision. Thank you I can and do bring these prayers before you in the name of Jesus. Amen.

Think on this: What is your focus? What do you look at most of the time? Does it enhance or tear down your faith walk? If the Holy Spirit has convicted you about not focusing on what God has for you, what would it mean for you to see only Jesus? Can you do it on your own? If not, whose help do you need, and how do you go about getting that help?

DAY 39

Are We There Yet?

"One of the mothers organized a field trip for the children in our neighborhood," Stan told me.

"To where?" I asked.

"Hawkins' Dairy, out on the road to Winston," he replied.

"When are they going?"

"We went yesterday."

"We?"

"Yeah," Stan replied, "I was a chaperone. I got to drive the van-load of excited children."

"How did it go?"

"Fabulous," he said. "They had a lot of fun, going, being there, and coming back. As you can imagine, we had only gone a few blocks from home when they started asking, 'Are we there yet?'"

We both laughed. Then I said, "Life is like that, isn't it? Always wondering if we've arrived, regardless of the destination."

"You're right, my friend," Stan responded. "I think the apostle Peter was writing about that in his second letter, but referring to our spiritual destination, as we walk with God."

"What's our spiritual destination?" I asked.

"The destination of manifesting Christian love," Stan replied. "Peter goes through the steps we are to follow, and we can talk about those another day. For now, I'd like to focus on the end goal Peter states: Christian love."

"Are you saying we should ask, 'Am I there yet?'"

"Yes," Stan replied. "It's essential for my faith walk with God to ask continually, 'Am I manifesting Christian love in my life?'"

"What if the answer is 'No'?" I asked.

"Time to find out why," Stan replied. "After all, the first-listed fruit of the Spirit is love. If I'm not manifesting Christian love as Peter writes, there's something missing. And that 'something' is usually easy to identify. It's the failure to get myself out of the way."

"Just like the first step in discipleship," I responded. "Deny self."

"Exactly," Stan said. "Get the old self out of the way, and let Christian love flow like a river!"

Bible verses to consider:
Now for this very reason also, applying all diligence, in your faith supply moral excellence, and in your moral excellence, knowledge; and in your knowledge, self-control, and in your self-control, perseverance, and in your perseverance, godliness; and in your godliness, brotherly kindness, and in your brotherly kindness, Christian love. 2 Peter 1:5-7.

By this all men will know that you are My disciples, if you have love for one another. John 13:35.

But the fruit of the Spirit is love.... Galatians 6:22.

Prayer: Thank you, Father, for so loving the world that you gave Jesus, so that all who believe will have life eternally with you when it's time. Thank you, Father, for personally loving me. Thank you for sending the Holy Spirit, whose fruit is love, to live within me so I will manifest your love in my life. I confess that too often I do not manifest that love. Forgive me, Father, and help me to change, so that I can truly show your unending love to a watching world. I want people to know that I am a disciple of Jesus, so that they will be drawn to Him. Thank you I can and do bring these prayers before you in His name. Amen.

Think on this: Christian love is the destination of your life. What is it like to be on that journey? Do you see evidence in your life that you are moving toward that goal? Why or why not? Are you where you think God would like you to be? What will it look like to "have arrived" at that destination?

DAY 40

Blessed with the Right Answer

"In Matthew's gospel," Stan began, "Jesus presented a question that I think is easily the single most important question a person can be asked."

"Wow," I responded. "That's quite a statement. What was the question?"

"Jesus asked His disciples, 'Who do you say that I am?' He asked me that question, and He asks each one of us. Our answer determines where we go when our time here is completed."

"Did the disciples get it right?" I asked.

"Matthew only records what Peter said, and yes, he got it right. He said that Jesus is the Christ, the Son of the living God."

"Did Matthew record how Jesus responded?"

"Yes, and it's very significant for every person who follows Jesus."

"What's that?" I asked.

"Jesus told Peter he was blessed by God to have the right answer. Peter hadn't come up with that amazing truth on his own. God revealed it to him."

"So how does that relate to you and me?"

"We've been blessed in the same way," Stan replied. "God has opened our eyes to see and understand that Jesus is the Christ, the Redeemer who accomplished for us what we could never have accomplished on our own."

"And God has enabled us to accept His gift of life eternally with Him?" I asked.

"Exactly!" Stan responded. "It's a free and gracious gift. Couldn't earn it; had to accept it. And think how blessed we are, on this side of eternity, to grow in an ever-deepening knowledge of God."

"While we wait for the train," I added. "So we're blessed for both sides of eternity, because God shows us the right answer to the question, 'Who is Jesus?'"

"Amen to that, my friend," Stan replied. "Blessing upon blessing, for which I express my gratitude every day!"

Bible verses to consider:
He said to them, "But who do you say that I am?" And Simon Peter answered and said, "Thou art the Christ, the Son of the living God." And Jesus answered and said to him, "Blessed are you, Simon Barjona, because flesh and blood did not reveal this to you, but My Father who is in heaven." Matthew 16:15-17.

Prayer: Thank you, Father, for blessing me with the right answer to Jesus' question, "Who do you say that I am?" Thank you for opening me to see and accept the truth, and for the assurance of life eternally with you when my time here is done. Thank you also for showing me what you have for me to be and do while I wait for the train. Please help me follow your lead as you use me to help others find the right answer to the most important question. Thank you I can and do bring these prayers before you in the name of Jesus. Amen.

Think on this: Have you been asked the most important question? If yes, how did you answer? Have you ever asked an unbeliever who they think Jesus is? Why or why not? What does it take for an unbeliever to know the answer? How can you pray for others who don't yet know who Jesus is?

DAY 41

One Size Fits All—or Not

"My wife and I are getting ready for a trip," Stan said. "There may be some rain where we're going, so we need to pack rain gear. I was looking at an online catalog and saw some ponchos that were described as 'one size fits all.'"

"That's pretty normal, isn't it?" I responded.

"Yeah, I suppose," Stan replied, "but there's a whole lot of difference in the size between me and my wife. She's petite and I'm not!"

"So the same poncho will fit each of you much differently."

"Exactly," Stan said. "And there's a spiritual lesson here."

"About ponchos?" I asked.

"Not ponchos," Stan replied, "but about one size fitting all."

"Let's have it," I said.

"When a person accepts the finished work of Christ on the cross and is redeemed for all of eternity, the Bible says that person is granted a robe of righteousness."

"A robe of righteousness?"

"Yeah," Stan said, "it means getting Christ's righteousness. So when God looks at me, He sees the righteousness of Jesus. With that robe given to each redeemed believer, it's clearly true that one size does fit all. Each person who puts on that robe finds it fits perfectly, and he or she is ready to step into eternity properly dressed when the time comes."

"Is there a difference for this side of eternity?" I asked.

"Yes. One size does not fit all on this side. We aren't intended to be alike and do the same things. God has different roles for each of us to fill. What God has for me to be and do is perfectly fitted for me, but that doesn't mean it's the same for you."

"Well," I replied, "if it's not the same for each person, how am I supposed to find out what it is for me?"

"Ask Him," Stan said. "As a believer, you have God's Holy Spirit. He is in you to guide, help, and counsel you in all things. And I can assure you He is ready, willing and able to help you find out what God has for you to be and to do while you wait for the train!"

"In other words, His plans always fit?"

"That's right," Stan said. "Each person who has settled his or her eternal destination is to find their intended role on this side of eternity. And I can tell you it's not a one-size-fits-all for this side."

Bible verses to consider:
I put on righteousness, and it clothed me; my justice was like a robe and a turban. Job 29:14.

He made Him who knew no sin to be sin on our behalf, that we might become the righteousness of God in Him. 2 Corinthians 5:21.

Work out your salvation with fear and trembling; for it is God who is at work in you, both to will and to work for His good pleasure. Philippians 2:12-13.

Prayer: Thank you, Father, for clothing me with the righteousness of Christ for when I step into eternity to be with you. Thank you for your provision through Jesus and His finished work on the cross. Thank you that you allowed me to accept your gracious free gift. Now that my eternal destination with you is settled, I know that you intend my life here to be different. I give you all of me to mold, shape, and transform exactly as you want, for your purposes. Thank you for wanting to use me in ways perfectly fitted for me. Please open me to see all you have for me to be and to do while you keep me here. Help me always to obey. Thank you I can and do bring all these prayers before you in the name of Jesus. Amen.

Think on this: Do you have Christ's robe of righteousness for when you step into eternity? If so, what do you think it means for your remaining time this side of eternity? How can you know what God has for you in the meantime? If you have not yet found what God has for you, do you know how to find out? Is that something you want to do? Why or why not?

DAY 42

The Basics of Discipleship: Denying Self

"Morning, Stan," I said as I sat down across from him. "I've got a question for you."

"What's up?" he replied.

"A while back, we talked a bit about the whole idea of discipleship."

"We did," Stan said. "We talked about it being optional. God wants it, but He will not force anyone to be a disciple."

"I've been focusing on the first part of what Jesus said," I replied, "about what I have to do to follow Him."

"The part about denying self?" Stan asked.

"That's right," I replied, "and I'm a little confused. How am I supposed to deny myself? I exist. How can I deny myself right out of existence? Is that what Jesus is talking about?"

"Yes and no," Stan replied. "I think Jesus is clearly telling me to deny myself, but it doesn't mean I am to deny I exist as a human being."

"So what am I supposed to deny?"

"I think it means I am to give up or abandon everything about me that is contrary to the new life God has given me in Christ."

"Like being something new or different from what I was before?" I asked.

"Exactly," Stan said. "That's the new life in Christ I am to manifest. And I can't manifest a new life if the old life is in the way."

"So," I replied, "deny the old self right out of existence? Is that what you are saying?"

"You got it, my friend," Stan said. "But remember we are apt to forget. Just because I get something one day doesn't mean I've got it for every day."

"You've said before that discipleship is a life-long process," I said.

"It is. We can't learn what it means to deny self in a day, a week, or a year. You and I are only touching the beginning. I have been on my faith walk for a long time. If I'm open to learning, the Holy Spirit has something every single day, hour, and minute for me to learn about denying self."

Bible verses to consider:
If anyone wishes to come after Me, let him deny himself.... Luke 9:23; Matthew 16:24.

And put on the new self, which in the likeness of God has been created in righteousness and holiness of the truth. Ephesians 4:24.

Or do you not know that your body is a temple of the Holy Spirit who is in you, whom you have from God, and that you are not your own? For you have been bought with a price: therefore glorify God in your body. 1 Corinthians 6:19-20.

Prayer: Thank you, Father, for wanting to be first in my life. Thank you for showing me that for you to be first, I cannot be first, that I have to deny myself by getting out of your way. I confess that too often I choose to exalt myself over you. Please forgive me of that foolishness. And please, Father, help me follow every step of your lead in truly denying myself so that you and you alone are on the throne of my life. Thank you I can and do bring these prayers before you in the name of Jesus. Amen.

Think on this: Exalting self is what the world has for us to do. Denying self is the first step in discipleship. What does it look like to deny what you want to be or do apart from God, so He can have full access to you? Have you made that choice? Is it enough to choose once, or is it a matter of choosing continually? If it's a continual choice, how does the Holy Spirit help? Does it involve surrendering to His lead? What would that look like in your life?

DAY 43

The Basics of Discipleship: Taking Up Your Cross

"Well," Stan began, "we've talked a little about discipleship being a choice for each of us."

"We have," I replied. "God wants it, but He's not going to force the issue."

"And," Stan continued, "we've opened the subject of the first step of discipleship."

"Denying self," I said. "So far, the part that's really struck me is that it's a life-long process."

"Right," Stan replied. "It's just like what we talked about earlier: not ever assuming I am a 'mature' Christian."

"Maturing, not mature," I said with a smile.

"Same thing with discipleship," Stan replied. "It's a continuing process for as long as God keeps me on this side of eternity. I'm growing, not grown!"

"When I was reading what Jesus' said next, there was something that really concerned me."

"What's that?" Stan asked.

"He says I have to 'take up my cross.' I don't understand what that means. Am I supposed to be physically crucified? I can't do that! Or does it mean something else? What is my 'cross?' And while I was reading Matthew's gospel, I noticed some tiny type next to the verse. It referred to a similar one in Luke's gospel. I looked that one up and noticed that Jesus adds that I am to take up my cross 'daily.'"

"You've done some looking into this," Stan replied. "Good for you! You have some great questions. I had the same ones when I was first starting down the discipleship path. I wondered what this 'take up my cross' thing was all about."

"Any conclusions?" I asked.

"For me," Stan replied, "it's a question of availability. I am to be available to God for whatever He has in mind for me to be and do. After I have denied self, by setting aside what I want to do apart from God, I must choose to 'take up' what God has for me. Whatever it is."

"Take up," I replied, "as in choosing. Is that it?"

"That's right, my friend," Stan said. "I'm not to sit here empty, having denied myself. No, I am to choose to be filled up with what God has for me to be filled up with. And," he added, "the 'daily' part that Luke includes is, I think, absolutely crucial for my faith walk. If I don't choose each day to be available for whatever God has for me, I'll be choosing to be filled back up with self."

"When Jesus says 'daily,' how many days does He mean?"

"As many as you have," Stan replied. "For as long as God chooses to keep you on this side of eternity, before you know it's time to go to the station to board the train."

Bible verses to consider:
If anyone wishes to come after Me, let him deny himself, and take up his cross.... Matthew 16:24.

If anyone wishes to come after me, let him deny himself, and take up his cross daily.... Luke 9:23.

And He went a little beyond them, and fell on His face and prayed, saying, "My Father, if it is possible, let this cup pass from Me; yet not as I will, but as Thou wilt. Matthew 26:39.

Prayer: Thank you, Father, that you sent your Son to go to the cross because of your love for the whole world, including me. Thank you that Jesus took up the cross in obedience to you and to your will. Thank you for wanting me to do the same, to take up my cross, whatever it is, in obedience to you. I confess I too often fall short of what you have for me to do. Please forgive me. And please help me follow every step of your lead so I am who you intend, doing what you intend. Thank you I can and do bring these prayers before you in the name of Jesus. Amen.

Think on this: If taking up your cross means being and doing whatever God intends for you, where are you with that? Are you where you think God wants you to be? Why or why not? If no, what changes would you like to see in your life? How will that happen? Do you agree that taking up your cross is a daily choice? Why or why not?

ETC is More Than Etcetera

As I sat across from Stan one morning, he asked, "Have I ever shared with you what I call ETC?"

"You mean etcetera? I asked. "Everyone knows what that means."

"No," he said. "It's more than etcetera. It's a shorthand way for me to remember something really important for my faith walk with God."

"Now you've got me curious," I said.

"Well," Stan replied, "it's an obvious fact that everything we do starts with our thoughts. What I think determines what I do. Good, bad, or somewhere in between."

"I can agree with that," I replied. "Thoughts determine what I say and what I do."

"So I have to be real careful about what thoughts I allow to influence me. When I think about anything in a way that is contrary to being like Christ, I need to capture that thought and not let it influence my words or actions. And one day, while I was having a conversation with God while journaling, I was given the image of a sticky note stuck on my forehead, in the front of my brain. It said ETC, for Every Thought Captive."

"That's a powerful image," I said. "And memorable."

"Every time I have an inappropriate thought about another person or my circumstances, or say a temptation comes into my mind, I stop and mentally see ETC. I then take that thought captive to the obedience of Christ."

"Does it work?" I asked.

"It does for me," Stan replied. "I need as many reminders as possible about who I am and who I am supposed to be in Christ. The sticky note thing reminds me of where God wants me to be, doing what He intends."

"Do you do it all the time?"

"I can't say I follow the process every time, but I can assure you that when I do, the Holy Spirit makes clear to me what I should be thinking about: God's perspective and purposes. And when my thoughts align with His, it makes a whole lot of difference in my actions. If I take every thought captive, and deliberately do it with Christ foremost in my mind, there's a much better chance I'll be living in obedience to Him."

"Sticky note with ETC," I replied. "I can remember that!"

Bible verses to consider:
For all have sinned and fall short of the glory of God. Romans 3:23.

We are taking every thought captive to the obedience of Christ. 2 Corinthians 10:5.

Prayer: Thank you, Father, for the ways in which you want to draw me ever closer to you. Thank you, too, for the reminders you bring to my thoughts. I confess that too often I let my thoughts roam freely, without paying attention to you. You know my tendency to have thoughts that are contrary to your will for me. Please help me follow and honor you even with my mind, so I that can live in obedience to your lordship. Thank you I can and do bring these prayers before you in the name of Jesus. Amen.

Think on this: What we do and what we say begins with a thought. Taking every thought captive to the obedience of Christ is the answer for doing and saying things that glorify God. It's not easy, but it's important. Where are you with that? Where would you like to be? How might having this sort of "mental sticky note" be helpful to you? Do you have anything similar to ETC that helps keep you on the path in your faith walk?

DAY 45

Being Remembered for Doing What You Could

"I was in Matthew's gospel earlier this morning," said Stan, "and came upon something that I long to hear Jesus say to me. I was so struck by it, I spent about a half hour journaling and praying about it."

"What was it?" I asked.

"Jesus was in Jerusalem, just before going to the cross to finish what the Father had sent Him to do. He and the disciples were having dinner at the home of a man called Simon the leper. I don't know if he was a friend of Jesus, a disciple, or what, but it doesn't matter who he was."

"What does matter about him?" I asked.

"Oh, it's not him," Stan replied. "It's about a woman who was there. A woman who brought some expensive perfume for Jesus. The woman, what she did, and what Jesus said about it, those are the important parts to me."

"What did she do?"

"She poured the perfume on Jesus. Some of the people who watched thought it was a dumb thing to do. They called it a big waste. They criticized the woman, saying the perfume could have been sold for money to give to the poor."

"Where did she get the perfume?" I asked.

"I don't know," Stan replied, "as I read about what she had done, that didn't stand out as being important."

"So what is important about this?" I asked.

“What Jesus said,” Stan responded. “What He says is always important, of course, but here there’s a special application for me. Something I long to hear Jesus say to or about me.”

“To or about you?”

“Definitely. Jesus took to task those who criticized the woman. He said she had done what she could and would be remembered forever.”

“Remembered forever,” I repeated. “Wow; how great would that be!”

“That would be great,” Stan replied, “but I like better the other things Jesus had to say: that the woman did what she could, implying that what she did was good. From this account, it occurs to me there are a couple questions I need the Holy Spirit to ask me on regular basis.”

“What questions?”

“Do I do what I can? And is it good?”

“You don’t mean working your way to heaven by doing good things?” I asked.

“Absolutely not,” Stan said. “I cannot work my way to heaven by anything I do, but only by accepting God’s gracious and free gift of salvation. No, the good things I do are to be done because I know where I’m going and am thankful for that assurance of salvation.”

“But do you think, when you get to heaven, God will ask those two questions?”

“Whether I did what I could, and was it good?” Stan replied.

“Yes,” I said. “Are you going to be asked that?”

“That’s a different subject for another day,” Stan replied, “but to give you a simple answer: yes!”

Bible verses to consider:
For when she poured this perfume upon My body, she did it to prepare Me for burial. Truly I say to you, wherever this gospel is preached in the whole

world, what this woman has done shall also be spoken of in memory of her. Matthew 26:12-13.

So then each one of us shall give an account of himself to God. Romans 14:12.

But they shall give account to Him who is ready to judge the living and the dead. 1 Peter 4:5.

Prayer: Thank you, Father, for your word and the voice of the Holy Spirit that show me how you want me to live now, before I step into eternity to be with you forever. I pray that you will be able to say of me what you said of the woman: that I did what I could in my relationship with You. I confess that I often do only what I want, apart from you. Please forgive me. And please help me follow every step of your lead, wherever you want to take me, so that I can serve you as you enable me. Thank you I can and do bring these prayers before you in the name of Jesus. Amen.

Think on this: It will be great to hear God say, "You did what you could, and it was good!" If you were to stand before Him in eternity right now, could He truly say that? If no, what changes do you need to make? What do you think it means to "do what you can?" How does "doing what you can" honor Jesus? Remember that it is not "doing" to get into heaven, but it is "doing" because you know that's where you are going.

DAY 46

Why are There so Many Hypocrites in the Church?

"There may have been a breakthrough with one of my neighbors," Stan said one morning.

"What kind of breakthrough?" I asked.

"Well," Stan replied, "for as long as we've been neighbors, I've invited him to worship services and other events at the church, but he always had an excuse for not accepting my invitation. Last night I invited him again to join us this Sunday, but he said he always plays golf with three friends on Sunday morning. So I told him there's a Saturday night service."

"What was his response to that?" I asked.

"He said he and his wife usually have dinner at their country club on Saturday night. And then he said, 'Besides, I don't want to go to church with a bunch of hypocrites.'"

"Wow," I replied, "he really said that? How did you react?"

"I asked him a question. I said, 'Do you know why there are so many hypocrites in the church?' He said, 'I don't know about that, I just know the church is full of people who say one thing and do another.' He said he really didn't want to be around them."

"Did you have a response?"

"I did," Stan replied. "I told him I thought the church is filled with hypocrites because that's all God has to work with. We're all hypocrites, whether we're in the church or not. I went on to tell him that the issue that really matters is where I want to spend eternity: in heaven with a bunch of hypocrites who have sought forgiveness and been forgiven, or in hell with a bunch of hypocrites who haven't bothered to seek forgiveness."

"Did he respond to that?" I asked.

"He just said, 'Oh, I hadn't thought about it in that way'."

"Do you think he will think about that?" I asked.

"That's my prayer," Stan replied. "And that God will open him to do more than just think about it!"

Bible verses to consider:
All have sinned and fall short of the glory of God, being justified as a gift by His grace, through the redemption which is in Christ Jesus. Romans 3:23-24.

And do you suppose this, O man, when you pass judgment upon those who practice such things and do the same yourself, that you will escape the judgment of God? Romans 2:3.

Prayer: Thank you, Father, for showing me my own hypocrisy in saying one thing and doing another. Please forgive all my hypocrisy, and help me follow your lead into an ever-deepening relationship with you, so that what I say and do agrees with what you have for me to be and to do. Thank you I can and do bring these prayers before you in the name of Jesus. Amen.

Think on this: Believers are the church. We are all that God has to work with on this side of eternity. Have you ever observed a Christian being a hypocrite? If so, what did that feel like? Have you ever observed yourself being a hypocrite? If no, maybe you need to look a bit closer! If, as this reading says, there are hypocrites in the church, what can be done about that? Do you believe the church would disappear if all the hypocrites left? Why or why not?

DAY 47

God's Activity: Looking at the Present

"Do you recall our conversation about looking backwards at God's activity, to see what He has done in a person's life?" asked Stan.

"I sure do," I responded. "We focused on seeing how we got to where we are in our relationship with God."

"Exactly," Stan replied. "And today I would like to focus on something that happened with another neighbor. It had to do with looking at God's activity in the present."

"What happened?" I asked.

"I've known him for a while," Stan said. "Although I've tried talking with him about Christianity, my faith, and that sort of thing, he has never been interested."

"Lot of people like that," I replied.

"There sure are," Stan said. "But I was pleasantly surprised recently. He approached me and was asking some questions that made me think God was presenting an opportunity for me to see His activity."

"In your neighbor's life?" I asked.

"Exactly," Stan replied. "And this again showed me how important it is for me to be aware of opportunities God gives, to really see what He is doing–and how He allows me to choose to be part of His work. If I don't recognize His activity in the present, there's no way for me to be involved with what He's doing."

"So you'd miss the opportunity to answer your neighbor's questions as deeply as you can, right?"

"Right," Stan said, "and if I miss that opportunity, my neighbor may miss the opportunity to have his life and eternal destination changed."

"Don't want that," I replied.

"No," Stan said, "and that's why I try to be on the continual lookout for how God may be moving, so I can join Him in what He is doing."

"Do you only see God moving when it involves people?" I asked.

"God is continually moving in circumstances as well as people," Stan said. "There are lots of opportunities to be a part of what God is doing. Just have to be open to seeing.

"Then choosing to join in!" I said.

"Yes," he said. "And regarding people, there is one person I especially have to pay attention to, so I can see God's activity."

"Who's that?"

"Me," he said. "Just look at the example of my neighbor. God was stirring his heart, moving him to approach me—and at the same time, God was active in my own heart and mind, saying in essence, 'Are you going to join Me here, or are you going to miss this opportunity?'"

Bible verses to consider:
Your people will volunteer freely in the day of Your power. Psalm 110:3.

But sanctify Christ as Lord in your hearts, always *being* ready to make a defense to everyone who asks you to give an account for the hope that is in you, but with gentleness and respect. 1 Peter 3:15.

Prayer: Thank you, Father, that you want me to see what you are doing, not only in the world around me, but in me. I confess that I often don't see because I don't look. Help me to moment-by-moment look to you, so I can understand and embrace what you are doing around and in me. As you show me what you are doing, please show me when I need to change, and how you want to use me. Thank you I can and do bring these prayers before you in the name of Jesus. Amen.

Think on this: Do you believe you can observe God's activity in and around you? Why or why not? If you see God's activity, what does it look like to join Him in what He is doing? How might you see God working in circumstances? In other people? In your own life? What would it look like to join God in what He wants to do? Is that something you would like? Is it something God would like?

DAY 48

Two Other Trinities

"I know," Stan began, "you're familiar with the Holy Trinity."

"Sure am!" I replied. "Father, Son, and Holy Spirit. Fabulous! There's a lot I don't understand, but God is helping me with that."

"He's working on me as well," Stan said. "But I want to point out two other trinities working to get in the way of the Holy Trinity."

"Two other trinities? What are you talking about, Stan?"

"The first that occurs to me is the trio of the world, the flesh, and the devil," he explained. "Those three are always at work trying to keep me distracted from what God has for me. Secondly," he added, "there's the trio of me, myself, and I."

"And that one also gets in the way?" I asked.

"Sure does," Stan replied. "Both of these so-called trinities, if I allow them, can have a real negative impact on my relationship with God. So much so that it might be fair to call them unholy trinities!"

"How am I supposed to deal with these other trinities?" I asked.

"First of all," Stan replied, "I think we need to recognize that this is a big subject. Virtually everything we talk about concerning our faith walk involves these things. The world, the flesh, and the devil are all part of living on this side of eternity."

"Just part of being here?"

"That's right. I'm constantly bombarded with temptations from this trinity. I have to stay aware. If I don't see their bombardment, I'm not keeping good watch. And that's exactly what the evil one wants!"

"Us not watching?" I asked.

"Exactly," Stan said. "And therefore not seeing and recognizing. Not only does Satan blind us to the truth of God, Satan can blind us to the truth of his own existence and activity."

"What about that second trinity?" I asked, "of me, myself and I?"

"That can be less obvious, but it's certainly clear to me when I pay close attention. That trinity is constantly getting in the way of being and doing what God intends."

"Keeping us from taking that first step in discipleship?"

"Well said, my friend! When I focus on the trinity of me, myself, and I, it's clear I'm exalting myself rather than denying myself. As I said, this is a big subject that's key to discipleship. Without denying myself, I'm not going anywhere in the direction God wants."

"Sounds like I need to constantly keep those two trinities in mind," I said. "But for how long?"

"For as long as God keeps you on this side of eternity," Stan replied.

"That seems like a lot of denying," I said. "I'm not sure I can do that."

"It's not easy," Stan said. "Same with most things that are worth doing. They aren't always easy, but the more we do them, the easier they get. Remember, we are never alone in the struggle: the perfect, powerful Trinity–Father, Son and Holy Spirit—is always ready, willing, and able to supply whatever help we need. We just have to ask!"

"Ready, willing and able," I repeated. "That's another encouraging trio!"

Bible verses to consider:
For our struggle is not against flesh and blood, but against the rulers, against the powers, against the world forces of this darkness, against the spiritual forces of wickedness in the heavenly places. Ephesians 6:12.

In the world you have tribulation, but take courage; I have overcome the world. John 16:33.

Work out your salvation with fear and trembling; for it is God who is at work in you, both to will and to work for His good pleasure. Philippians 2:12-13.

If anyone wishes to come after Me, let him deny himself, and take up his cross, and follow Me. Matthew 16:24.

Prayer: Thank you, God, that you are a holy Trinity, Father, Son and the Holy Spirit. You know how much I can struggle with the unholy trinities of the world, the flesh, and the devil, along with me, myself, and I. Thank you for providing all I need to deal with those unholy trinities. I confess that too often I choose not to reject them, because I choose to walk a path away from you. Please, Father, help me follow your lead so that you yourself, as the Holy Trinity, are at the center of my life. Thank you I can and do bring these prayers before you in the name of Jesus. Amen.

Think on this: The Holy Trinity is the heart of Christianity. What do you know about God the Father? The Son? The Holy Spirit? How can you learn more? How do the other "trinities" that Stan describes contrast with God's will for you? Do you struggle with these trinities? Do you know that the help you need is always available? Who can help you? How can you receive that help?

Getting Around the Congestion

"I drove over to Centerville the other day," I told Stan. "The traffic was an absolute mess right around Junction City."

"I know it sure can be," he responded. "A lot of people have moved out there. It's gotten really crowded and busy. I assume you didn't take the bypass that goes around Junction City."

"Bypass? I didn't know there was one. How would I have found it?"

"Well, it's not real easy to find, but if I had known you were going to Centerville, I could have given you directions."

"I wish I'd known," I said. "It would have saved me a lot of time."

"And a lot of frustration," Stan said. "You know, the whole idea of bypassing congestion has a lot of similarities to my faith walk with God."

"How so?"

"If I ask God for directions from point A to point B, whatever those points are, He always knows the best way to get there. But too often I don't ask the right questions, and then I experience what you did: I'm stuck in the congestion of life."

"Why don't you ask the right questions?"

"In one word: me. Me assuming I know what route to take, from where I am to where I want to be."

"How do you get directions from God?"

"Two distinct ways," said Stan.

"Which are what?" I asked.

"First, I need to spend time studying God's roadmap, which is the Bible. Secondly, I need to be in regular prayer, asking Him to help me bypass any congestion that gets in the way of walking with Him."

"He will do that?" I asked.

"Absolutely!" Stan exclaimed. "And I can save a lot of heartache, headache, frustration, and time if I choose to go His way instead of mine."

"Isn't that kind of what confession and repentance are all about?"

"You got it, my friend," he said.

Bible verses to consider:
The highway of the righteous is to depart from evil; he who watches his way preserves his life. Proverbs 16:17.

Thomas said to Him, "Lord, we do not know where You are going; how do we know the way?" Jesus said to him, "I am the way, and the truth, and the life; no one comes to the Father, but through Me." John 14: 5-6.

There is a way which seems right to a man, but its end is the way of death. Proverbs 14:12.

Prayer: Thank you, Father, for giving me free will to go whatever way I want, and for giving me the choice to choose the way you have for me. You know, and I know, the difficulties I get myself into by following my way, rather than yours. Please forgive all the times of such foolishness. I need and ask for all the help you can provide, to turn around so you can show me where I should go. Please help me follow your way, and not my own, in every aspect of my life. Thank you I can and do bring these prayers before you in the name of Jesus. Amen.

Think on this: Do you ever find yourself stuck in the congestion of life because you chose to go a different way than God had for you? Have you ever found out you were going completely in the wrong direction? If so, what did that feel like, and what did you do about it? How can you ask God for directions in the first place? Do you know how to study God's roadmap, the Bible? Do you ask for directions through prayer on a consistent basis? Why or why not? Do you believe God always knows the best way?

DAY 50

The Weeds of Life

"The family farm I grew up on," Stan began, "was quite a distance from anyone or anything. Whenever we wanted to go anywhere, it involved a drive."

"Dirt roads and all that?" I asked.

"That's right," Stan replied, "lots of dirt and dirt roads. And yesterday, for some reason, I recalled a time I was with my dad in his pickup truck. We drove by a neighbor's field, and my dad suddenly slowed down and stopped. He wasn't a spiritual person; at least he never talked about it. It's hard to imagine a farmer not having a deep appreciation of God, considering how magnificent God's creation is. But there was no evidence my dad had that kind of faith."

"So what happened when he stopped at the neighbor's field?"

"He unintentionally gave me a spiritual lesson, by saying something I never want God to say about me."

"What's that?" I asked.

"'Look at all those weeds,' he said. 'Jim sure doesn't pay much attention to being a farmer.'"

"Why would God say that to you, Stan?" I asked. "You're not a farmer."

"I'm not a farmer, but I'm sometimes inattentive to the weeds in my life."

"Weeds?"

"Yes; all the things that can disrupt the growth of good things in my faith walk. Can you imagine," he continued, "my heavenly Father 'driving by' my life with His Son and saying, 'Look at all those weeds–Stan's not paying attention to what he's doing as a Christian!'"

"That would be hard to hear," I responded. "You think that could really happen?"

"I do," Stan replied. "Satan just loves to spread his weed seeds and encourage germination and growth. Weeds will sprout up, grow, and choke out the good things we are to produce."

"Saying you're sometimes inattentive seems to imply you should be working. What kind of work are you talking about?"

"Certainly not working my way to heaven," Stan replied. "That's not possible. Salvation is only available through faith, by accepting God's free and gracious gift of Jesus' finished work on the cross."

"Well then, what kind of work is it?"

"Working out the salvation that has been worked in by God. Salvation is not the end of the story. I think it's just the beginning of what God intends for me to be doing while I wait for the train."

"Okay," I responded, "I don't work for my salvation, but I do work out my salvation. And an important part of that is watching out for weeds."

"Well said," Stan replied. "Because weeds are surely not what God wants Himself, or anyone, to see in my life, when they drive by, stop, and take a look!"

Bible verses to consider:
I passed by the field of the sluggard, and by the vineyard of the man lacking sense; and behold, it was completely covered with nettles, and its stone wall was broken down. When I saw, I reflected upon it; I looked and received instruction. "A little sleep, a little slumber, a little folding of the hands to rest," then your poverty will come as a robber, and your want like an armed man. Proverbs 24:30-34.

For by grace you have been saved through faith; and that not of yourselves, it is the gift of God; not as a result of works, that anyone should boast. Ephesians 2:8, 9.

Work out your salvation with fear and trembling. Philippians 2:12.

And the one on whom seed was sown among the thorns, this is the man who hears the word, and the worry of the world, and the deceitfulness of riches choke out the word, and it becomes unfruitful. Matthew 13:22.

Prayer: Thank you, Father, for your gracious and free gift of salvation through my acceptance of Christ's finished work on the cross. Thank you that you want me to work out the salvation you have worked in. I confess that too often I do not pursue that working out, because I choose to do what I want to do apart from you. Please forgive me. And please, Father, help me follow your lead so that the time I have on this side of eternity is dedicated to seeking, finding, receiving, and embracing all you have for me to be and to do. Help me see and remove the weeds growing in my life that choke out the good fruit you want to grow. Thank you I can and do bring these prayers before you in the name of Jesus. Amen.

Think on this: What are some of the weeds in your life? How did they get there? Do you want to get rid of them? If so, how can that happen? Is it possible to have a life without any weeds? Why or why not?

DAY 51

Discipleship is a Two-Way Street

After Ricky had refilled our coffee, Stan said, "You know, my friend, I want to thank you for all the ways you help me in the time we spend together."

"I help you?" I responded. "I thought all this time together was about you helping me, not the other way around."

"Oh, I don't think so," Stan replied. "And I think there's another angle to how discipleship is viewed."

"What's that?" I asked.

"It seems to me, if a discipling mentor gets to the point of thinking he or she is just the teacher, and not also the student, that person has started heading down the wrong road."

"Student? Teacher? I'm still not sure I understand."

"Discipleship is certainly about a more mature believer helping one who is less mature," Stan replied, "but the whole process of maturing grinds to a halt for both of them if the one who is supposedly more mature stops growing."

"I remember our discussion about that," I said, "how there's always room for further growth."

"That's right," Stan replied. "In our relationship, if I don't listen to you, wanting to know your perspective on what we're discussing, I'm heading in the wrong direction."

"But what if I don't have a perspective?" I asked.

"That's okay," Stan said. "You may not have a perspective that you can verbalize, but you certainly have questions. And I think questions actually are a perspective. The essential point concerning our time together is this: discipleship is a two-way street!"

"It goes both ways, then?"

"Exactly," Stan said. "If I start to view myself as sitting on a throne, dispensing what I think is knowledge, with no input from you, my role as your spiritual mentor has either ended or is heading in that direction."

"You often remind me," I said, "that Jesus described eternal life as knowing God the Father and Himself as the Son. If I can help you know God as much as you've helped me, I'll be very grateful."

"And I will continue to say 'Thank you,' my friend!"

Bible verses to consider:
I say to every one among you not to think more highly of yourself than you ought to think. Romans 12:3.

And this is eternal life, that they may know Thee, the only true God, and Jesus Christ whom Thou hast sent. John 17:3.

Prayer: Thank you, Father, for wanting me to mature as a believer. Thank you, too, for wanting me to help other people on their path to deeper maturity in their faith walk. Thank you that eternal life is the process of knowing you and your Son. Keep me from assuming I have nothing to learn from another believer, and please bring people into my life who can help me know you ever more deeply. Open me to hear and to listen to all you have to say through them. Thank you I can and do bring these prayers before you in the name of Jesus. Amen.

Think on this: Have you ever been in a discipling relationship? Is so, were you the one discipling or being discipled? What was the experience like? If you have never been in a discipling relationship, why? Do you agree that discipleship is a two-way street? Why or why not?

DAY 52

Let it Begin with Me

Stan had a unique question to open our time. "Do you think God needs any help?"

I thought for a moment, then said, "I guess the starting place for an answer is God's character. He's all-powerful, all-knowing, the Lord God Almighty. He surely doesn't need any help from anyone, including me."

"Pretty good starting place," Stan replied. "Thanks for that reminder. God can do whatever He wants, however, wherever and whenever He wants. But that's not the end of the story."

"Maybe 'need' is the wrong question?" I asked.

"I agree. While God doesn't need my help for anything," Stan replied, "I think He certainly desires it."

"Need versus desire?"

"Yes. Take, for example, what Matthew records, where Jesus was teaching His disciples how to pray."

"You mean the Lord's Prayer?"

"Yes. I've heard it called the disciples' prayer or the 'Our Father.' But what really matters is what Jesus is teaching us about the will of the Father being done on earth as in heaven. I like to put a sort of p.s. after that part."

"A p.s?"

"I like to pray 'Thy kingdom come. Thy will be done, on earth as it is in heaven–beginning with me.'"

"Beginning with me? What does that mean?"

"To me it means I'm surrendering all of me to all of God, so He can use me in what He wants to accomplish on earth. Whatever, whenever, wherever and however. I want to tell Him I am fully available."

"Maybe that's why," I said, "it so often seems that God's will isn't being done on earth. Maybe not enough people are willing to be used."

"That's a distinct possibility," Stan replied. "Why don't we see what we can do to help?"

Bible verses to consider:
And He withdrew from them about a stone's throw, and He knelt down and began to pray, saying, "Father, if Thou art willing, remove this cup from Me; yet not My will, but Thine be done." Luke 22:41-42.

Thy kingdom come. Thy will be done, on earth as it is in heaven. Matthew 6:10.

Prayer: Thank you, Father, for wanting your will and purposes to be done and accomplished on earth just as they are in heaven. I confess that too often I am not willing to be used by you. I am not available because I choose to be unavailable and because I am too busy doing what I want to do apart from you. Please forgive me and help me follow every step of your lead, so that your will is done on earth as in heaven, beginning and continuing with me. Thank you I can and do bring these prayers before you in the name of Jesus. Amen.

Think on this: Do you believe God wants to use you for His will to be done on earth? Why or why not? What does it look like to be involved with God in accomplishing His purposes in your life? How about in your family? Your neighborhood and even beyond? What changes might happen in the world if more people asked to be used to accomplish His will? Is this a part of what discipleship means?

DAY 53

Pure as Maple Syrup

As we waited for Ricky to take our order, Stan said, "I definitely know what I want today."

"Let me guess," I said. "Pancakes?"

"Blueberry pancakes," he said. "My very favorite. These guys really know how to make them, with all those sweet berries in the batter."

"Are you still going to add this?" I said, picking up the syrup bottle. "It says, 'Vermont maple, one hundred percent pure.'"

Stan smiled, then looked thoughtful. "You know, that's what I want to be: one hundred percent pure."

"Think it will happen?" I asked.

"Not on this side of eternity. But that's no reason not to make it a priority, for as long as God keeps me here."

"You know," I said, "I sometimes think about that. But I fail so often that I tend to think, 'What's the use in trying?'"

"When I think like that," Stan countered, "and I certainly have many times, I know I'm headed in the wrong direction. In fact, I'm delighting Satan with that kind of thinking. He just loves it when Christians give up."

"So you've also felt like a spiritual failure at times?" I asked.

"More times than I care to admit. But if I confess every failure and ask God for His help with my repentance, He picks me up, dusts me off, bandages my wounds, and sets me back on His path towards what He has for me to be and to do."

"You've said before that's what confession and repentance are all about. Admitting my faults and failures. Asking God for His help."

"And then embracing all He has for me," Stan said. "He wants me to have pure thoughts, pure motives, and pure actions. And He will do all that is necessary, if I will just ask Him and get myself out of His way. Then, through the Holy Spirit, He can do exactly what He alone is capable of doing!"

"Make you one hundred percent pure?" I asked.

"Perfect purity is not attainable in our fallen world. Jesus is the only one who ever lived a sinless life. He asked His Father to send the Holy Spirit to live within each believer, to live the life God intends. I just need to get me out of the way, so the Holy Spirit can do what He is in me to do."

"And every step in that direction pleases God," I reminded him.

When Ricky showed up with the blueberry pancakes, Stan picked up the bottle of maple syrup and poured on a generous portion. "Pure delight!" he said. "Let's thank the Lord for His provision and get down to business!"

Bible verses to consider:
How can a young man keep his way pure? By keeping it according to God's word. Psalm 119:9.

All have sinned and fall short of the glory of God. Romans 3:23.

He made Him who knew no sin to be sin on our behalf, that we might become the righteousness of God in Him. 2 Corinthians 5:21.

As obedient children, do not be conformed to the former lusts which were yours in your ignorance, but like the Holy One who called you, be holy yourselves also in all your behavior; because it is written, "You shall be holy for I am holy." 1 Peter 1:14-16.

Prayer: Thank you, Father, for wanting my ways to be pure and holy. You know my heart and my desire to be pure in all my thoughts, words, and actions. And you know how difficult it is for me and how often I fail. I give you all my failings and shortcomings and ask you to forgive them. Please move in and through me in accordance with your will. Help me to be as pure as you want. Please help me to get myself out of your way so you can do what you want in and through me. Thank you I can and do bring all these prayers before you in the name of Jesus. Amen.

Think on this: What does purity look like to you? What do you think it looks like from God's perspective? Is purity attainable? Why or why not? What does it look like to be committed to living a pure life? What does the world think of such efforts? Does it matter to you what the world thinks? Why or why not? Do you think failing to live a pure and holy life is the end of the story? Why or why not? Where do confession and repentance fit in?

DAY 54

Connected to What and How?

Stan was looking around the restaurant as if anticipating something. "Are you looking for someone?" I asked.

"No, sorry. Just observing. Have you ever noticed how people spend so much time looking at their cell phones?"

"I have," I replied. "So many are continuously connected. It's almost like an addiction."

"Continuously connected," Stan repeated. "That's a good way to describe it." He paused, then added, "Think how great it would be if that many people sought to be continually connected with God."

"Is that possible?"

"Not only possible, but I think that's what God intends."

"For each of us to be continually connected? You really believe that?"

"I do," Stan responded. "And I think the apostle Paul addresses that. He wrote about being devoted to prayer and about praying without ceasing."

"So prayer is not just for prayer meetings," I said.

"Of course, those kind of get-togethers are great, but I believe that prayer is intended to be an ongoing conversation with God. It should be a lifestyle of constant contact with God—to use your phrase, continually connected."

"If that's true," I responded, "won't prayer get in the way of getting anything else done?"

"Nope," Stan said emphatically. "If I am constantly and continuously connected with the Lord God Almighty, His Holy Spirit will lead me with assurance that I am doing all He has for me to do. Modern technology is a great way to connect with other people, but it has to be kept in proper perspective. I can't let the modern outweigh the age-old provision of connection with God."

Bible verses to consider:

Devote yourselves to prayer. Colossians 4:3.

Pray without ceasing. 1 Thessalonians 5:17.

Prayer: Thank you, Father, that you provide the way to be continuously connected to you through prayer. I confess that way too often I do not stay connected with you as you intend, because I choose to be connected elsewhere. Please forgive me. And please, Father, give me a greater desire to stay connected with you, outweighing my desire to connect to other things and people. You are high above everything else in this world. Thank you I can and do bring these prayers before you in the name of Jesus. Amen.

Think on this: Today's electronics provide virtually constant connectivity. Some say that such connectivity is not healthy, because it takes our focus off more important things. Do you agree or disagree? Do you think you are connected with God as fully as He wants? If no, do you know how to increase that connectivity? What do you think it means to pray without ceasing? Do you want to do that?

DAY 55

Keep from Getting Sidetracked

"As I turned onto Main Street this morning," Stan began, "I was reminded of a pastor we once had."

"How so?" I asked.

"The pastor was very fond of saying, 'The main thing is to keep the main thing the main thing'."

"What did he mean by that?"

"It depended on his subject," Stan replied. "But his point was always the same: keep focused on what God considers important, and don't lose track of it."

"You have an example?" I asked.

"Sure do," Stan replied. "Let's say you're thinking about how happy you are with your church. Say you're not crazy about the type of music that's presented, and you're thinking about finding a different church with music more to your liking."

"Okay," I said, "what about it?"

"My pastor's point would be this: the main thing to focus on is not the music, but on whether or not the truth of the Gospel is presented."

"I'd say that's the main thing for any Christian church to focus on."

"I agree," said Stan, "and it's also the most important thing for me to focus on. Satan just loves to get me sidetracked into looking only at less important things."

"Or completely unimportant things," I added. "You've said before that Satan hates it when the gospel is presented."

"He also hates it when Christians are serious about their Christianity, when they are serious about pursuing spiritual maturity through transformation. So," he continued, "I need to be mindful that Satan is delighted if he can distract me by focusing on the style of music, the color of the carpet, the pastor's clothes, the hair style of the person sitting in front of me, or anything else that's really not important."

"How does a person keep the focus on the main thing?" I asked.

"First I have to know what God considers the main thing: His free and gracious gift of eternal salvation through Jesus. And after accepting that gift, I need to know what God considers the next main thing."

"Which is what?" I asked.

"Working out that salvation," Stan replied.

"By the three steps of being a disciple," I said, and Stan nodded as I named them. "Denying self whatever that looks like, taking up my cross whatever that involves, and following Him wherever He might want to lead."

Bible verses to consider:
We preach Christ crucified. 1 Corinthians 1:23.

Set your minds on the things *that are* above, not on the things that are on earth. For you have died, and your life is hidden with Christ in God. Colossians 3:2-3.

And He was saying to them all, "If anyone wishes to come after Me, let him deny himself, and take up his cross daily, and follow Me." Luke 9:23.

Prayer: Thank you, Father, for giving your only begotten Son to provide the way for eternal salvation through His life, death, and resurrection. Your free and gracious gift of salvation is the most important thing ever to come into my life. Thank you that you want the truth of salvation presented throughout the entire world. Help your church keep the focus on the truth of Christ crucified, and help us recognize when Satan is trying to turn our focus to unimportant things. May all who call on your name stay focused on your main thing. I ask the same thing for myself, that I would stay focused on what you intend for me while you keep me on this side of eternity. Thank you I can and do bring these prayers before you in the name of Jesus. Amen.

Think on this: What is the main thing in your life? What about the main thing in your relationship with God? Do your top priorities and concerns match God's? Why or why not? What would it look like for your "main thing" to agree with God's? Is that possible? If so, do you know how that can happen?

DAY 56

What Does Your Boat Look Like?

"You remember the story about Peter walking on the water?" Stan asked.

"A little bit," I responded. "If I remember correctly, it's an amazing event that followed two other amazing events. One was the feeding of the five thousand. The other was Jesus Himself walking on the water."

"You're right," Stan replied. "And I was looking at Peter's water-walking adventure earlier this morning. It has some lessons for me and my dry-land walk with God."

"Such as what?"

"First," Stan said, "what happened with Peter is not limited to a boat. It applies to any situation I'm in. God may want me to leave where I am, to be somewhere else. Second, I need to have my spiritual ears open so I hear whenever Jesus tells me, 'Come.' If I'm not paying attention, I may miss His invitation or command."

"Can't follow Jesus' word unless I hear what He has to say," I said.

"That's it," Stan replied. "And the third lesson is to do what Peter did: get out of the boat. If I don't move myself out of whatever situation I'm in, there's little chance God will do what He wants to do. While I acknowledge that God can do whatever He wants, I don't expect Him to grab me and pull me out of my 'boat.' He wants me to choose to do what's necessary. And then follow up that choice with actually doing it."

"You mean don't just say I'm choosing without acting on that choice?"

"Yes," Stan said, "for me to choose but not act, makes it a pretty empty choice. And Peter didn't get out of the boat and start walking in any old direction. He walked toward Jesus. Same for me."

"So," I replied, "this whole story of Peter, the boat, and the water, seems to concern discipleship. Listening and acting so that I don't miss the wonderful opportunity of following Him wherever He wants to lead."

"You've got that right, my friend. Choosing to get out of the boat is like denying self. Then the actual getting out of the boat is like taking up my cross. Thirdly, walking on the water towards Jesus is like following Him."

"It seems to me," I replied, "that the ideas of discipleship and choosing to be a disciple are just about everywhere I look."

"Same for me," Stan said. "I just have to have my eyes open!"

Bible verses to consider:
And He said, "Come!" And Peter got out of the boat, and walked on the water and came toward Jesus. Matthew 14:29.

If anyone wishes to come after Me, let him deny himself, and take up his cross daily, and follow Me. Luke 9:23.

Prayer: Thank you, Father, for the story of Peter's walk on the water, and how it applies to the faith walk you have for me on dry land. Thank you for wanting me to follow you wherever you want to lead. I know that following you may require leaving a comfortable place so that I can find my ultimate comfort in you. Please help me follow your lead to be where you want, doing what you want. Thank you I can and do bring these prayers before you in the name of Jesus. Amen.

Think on this: Have you been in a situation where you sensed God was calling you to leave, but you didn't want to? If so, what happened? If you were not able to get 'out of the boat,' why not? If you were able, did it turn out the way you expected? Why or why not? What could have made it different? What did you learn from the experience?

DAY 57

Proof of Receipt

"When we are finished with our time together this morning," Stan said, "I need to stop by the post office. I hope I don't forget."

"What do you need to do there?"

"In my mailbox yesterday, there was a notice of a registered letter. I'm not sure what it's all about, but I do know I need to show the notice, and I have to sign before they give me the letter. They need some sort of proof of receipt."

"Sounds important," I responded. "I'll try to remind you."

"Thanks," Stan replied. "You know, there are some real parallels between signing for this letter and my faith walk through the Holy Spirit."

"How so?"

"Jesus told His disciples He would ask His Father to send the Holy Spirit to be their Helper. He also told His disciples to receive the Holy Spirit. And the New Testament letters contain a lot about how the Holy Spirit is to be manifested in and through me."

"So," I replied, "the Holy Spirit has to be received before He can be manifested. Is that what you are saying?"

"That's right," Stan said. "My life should show I have received the Holy Spirit. I should manifest His presence by bearing fruit. In other words, He wants my life to be proof of receipt."

"And if it's not?" I asked.

"I need to take some time to examine what's going on," Stan replied, "as well as checking to see what's not going on. After all," he concluded, "it doesn't just happen. As with everything in my faith walk, choices are involved. If I choose to get me out of the way so the Holy Spirit can do what He intends, the proof will be there. If I don't, it won't."

Bible verses to consider:
He came to His own, and those who were His own did not receive Him. But as many as received Him, to them He gave the right to become children of God, even to those who believe in His name, who were born not of blood, nor of the will of the flesh, nor of the will of man, but of God. John 1:11-13.

Receive the Holy Spirit. John 20:22.

But the fruit of the Spirit is love, joy, peace, patience, kindness, goodness, faithfulness, gentleness, and self-control. Galatians 5:22-23.

Prayer: Thank you, Father, for sending your only Son into the world to atone for my sin. Thank you He has taken care of my separation from you, and I can look forward with assurance to spending eternity with you when it's time. Thank you, too, for answering Jesus' request that you send the Holy Spirit to help, counsel, guard, and guide me during the time I have left on this side of eternity. I confess that too often I do not get myself sufficiently out of His way so He can do all you intend in and through me. Help me to follow your every step, giving you unhindered access to my life so that it is proof I have received the Holy Spirit. Thank you I can and do bring these prayers before you in the name of Jesus. Amen.

Think on this: Have you received the free gift of salvation through Christ's finished work? If no, why? If you have, you also have the Holy Spirit. Have you invited Him into every part of your life? How might others see "proof of receipt?" What do you think it means to receive the Holy Spirit? Is the fruit of the Spirit (Galatians 5:22-23) being manifested in and through you as God wants? If no, what can be done about it? Can you do it on your own?

DAY 58

Have You Checked the Box?

"I did something last night I've never done before," Stan said.

"What's that?" I asked.

"I'm not a big internet guy," he responded, "but I checked out a blog."

"Why?"

"A friend had forwarded an email that was a Christian devotional. I really liked what I read, so I went to the blog it came from."

"Find anything interesting?" I asked.

"I did," Stan said. "Lots of good stuff I really enjoyed, with helpful insights."

"How often is new material posted?"

"Looks like there's a new devotional just about every day," Stan replied.

"So, will you be going back every day to see what's new?"

"It'll be easy now," he said, "because each new posting will automatically get sent to me."

"How's that happen?" I asked.

"At the bottom of the first blog page, there was a box that said 'Follow.' I checked it and typed in my email address."

"That sounds great," I replied. "Good for you. If you think I'd like it, send me the information so I can sign up, too."

"I will," Stan responded. "I definitely think I'm going to enjoy reading each devotional. But there's something even better for me to follow."

"What's that?" I asked.

"God in Christ," Stan said.

"That third step in discipleship," I added.

"That's right. Following a blog each day is fine, but, for me, what God has to say directly through His word and His Spirit is better. This doesn't come automatically like an email, but when I'm open to receiving, I hear from Him."

Bible verses to consider:
And He was saying to them all, "If anyone wishes to come after Me, let him deny himself, and take up his cross daily, and follow Me." Luke 9:23.

Follow Me. John 21:19.

Prayer: Thank you, Father, for wanting me to follow you wherever you want to lead, whatever the cost. Thank you for allowing me to follow you. There is so much in this world to lead me away from you. Please help me keep away from all that leads me away from you. And please help me choose to follow only you. Thank you I can and do bring these prayers before you in the name of Jesus. Amen.

Think on this: Who and/or what do you follow? Why? Can you say you follow God and whatever He has for you? Why or why not? When you choose to follow God, there are costs involved. What are some of those costs? Might those costs be too great for you? Why or why not? If you aren't following God as closely as you think He wants, do you know how to change that?

DAY 59

The New Head Guy

"I heard that the church on Elm and Grove has a new pastor," I said to Stan one morning.

"I have a friend who's one of their elders," he replied. "He said the previous pastor left to pursue a new calling. The elders then searched, found and hired someone. I actually had the opportunity to meet him at a community reception."

"Nice fellow?" I asked.

"Very. He seems like a great choice for the church. Easy going, gentle, fun, and most of all, he passed the test."

"Test?" I asked. "What test?"

"Well," Stan said, "rightly or wrongly, I'm prone to ask people questions just to test where they are in their walk with God."

"And you did that with the new pastor?" I asked a bit skeptically.

"I did," Stan replied. "As I shook his hand I said, 'So you're the new head guy.'"

"How did he respond to that?"

"He looked at me for a few seconds, then said, 'I'm just the new pastor. But I know and work for the One who is the head of the church, Jesus Christ."

"That's a great response," I said. "And humble."

"I agree. I really shook his hand after that and told him I was delighted to meet him and welcome him to our community."

"Sounds like the elders made a real good choice."

"I agree," said Stan. "Pastors and elders are to help lead the flock under the headship of Christ, but if they begin to think they are the head or heads of the church, I think trouble is brewing and Satan is smiling. Jesus is the head of His church. Period."

Bible verses to consider:
And He put all things in subjection under His feet, and gave Him as head over all things to the church, which is His body, the fulness of Him who fills all in all. Ephesians 1:22-23.

And He is the image of the invisible God, the first-born of all creation. Colossians 1:15.

Prayer: Thank you, Father, for giving your Son to be the head of the church. Thank you, too, that He is the head of every aspect of my life. Please forgive the times I try to assert headship over and above Him. I ask for your hand of blessing on the church, so that pastors, elders, and leaders will truly and continually submit to your headship and do what you have for them to do, denying themselves, taking up their crosses, and following you. I ask for your help in building and maintaining a healthy church in accordance with your will. Thank you I can and do bring all these prayers before you in the name of Jesus, your chosen Head of your church. Amen.

Think on this: Are you part of the body of Christ, the church? If so, who do you consider the head to be? If you are not part of a local church, why not? Do you agree that recognizing Jesus' headship is an essential part of discipleship? Why or why not? Can you say that Jesus is the head of your life? What does that look like?

DAY 60

Getting to Know the Author

"One of my neighbors is the owner and operator of that little bookstore over on Grand, just off Main Street," said Stan.

"I know that one," I said. "Little Box Bookstore."

"Nice lady," Stan said. "Owning a small bookstore can be a tough business these days, but she seems to have carved out a niche and is doing fine. She had an event the other day, where an author was reading from his new book. People could ask questions, and, of course, there was an opportunity to buy a signed copy!"

"Of course," I replied. "Did you buy one?"

"I did. And my neighbor invited my wife and me to dinner with the author after the store closed."

"Well, that was sure nice," I said.

"It was a great time. I got to know him more than just casually. Very interesting fellow! I'm looking forward to reading his book. You know," Stan added, "it's similar to my experience with God and His book."

"How so?"

"There's a difference between knowing what's in the Bible itself, and knowing the Author Himself. God's book isn't just a bunch of words on pages; it's not just a collection of nice thoughts and helpful suggestions. No, the Bible consists of words from God's heart. And He wants to write them on mine."

"And I guess you're thinking that can't happen," I said, "unless I choose to get to know Him by spending time in His word and in His presence."

"You know me pretty well by now," Stan smiled. "That is what I'm thinking. If I want to have an ever-deepening relationship with God, I have to take steps beyond just meeting Him. I have to get to know Him."

"Knowing God the Father and Jesus the Son," I recalled for us both, "is what Jesus said about eternal life."

"Yes," Stan concluded. "He said that is what eternal life is. And I sure don't want to miss it!"

Bible verses to consider:

And this is eternal life, that they may know Thee, the only true God, and Jesus Christ whom Thou hast sent. John 17:3.

You shall therefore impress these words of mine on your heart and on your soul; and you shall bind them as a sign on your hand, and they shall be as frontals on your forehead. Deuteronomy 11:18.

Do not let kindness and truth leave you; bind them around your neck, write them on the tablet of your heart. Proverbs 3:3.

Prayer: Thank you, Father, for wanting me to know you and for making yourself available to be known. I confess I often choose to do what I want to do apart from you. Please forgive me. And please, Father, help me follow every step of your lead into an ever-deepening relationship. Please build in me the desire to have you place on my heart what is on yours. Thank you I can and do bring these prayers before you in the name of Jesus. Amen.

Think on this: Do you think it's possible to know God? Why or why not? If yes, do you know Him as well as you would like? How do you think He wants to use His book in your relationship with Him? Do you know what it means to have His word written on your heart? If not, how can you find out?

DAY 61

Keeping with Repentance

"Have you read Luke's account of John the Baptist?" asked Stan.

"Yes," I said, "I recall he was in the wilderness."

"That's right. At the Jordan River, preaching and baptizing."

"Did he have anything to say that long ago that has any application for today?"

"He sure did!" Stan responded. "John told the people then, and is telling me today, to 'bring forth fruits in keeping with your repentance.' To me, that's a clear statement that my life should be examined on a regular basis to see where I am on the repentance scale."

"The repentance scale?" I asked. "What do you mean by that? And who's doing the examination?"

"The Holy Spirit is the One doing the examination," he said. "If I've confessed and repented, my life should be a whole lot different from what it was before. If it's not, it's time to find out why. If there's no fruit in my life in accordance with what I said when I repented, it's likely my repentance wasn't real. And maybe my confession wasn't either. I need to ask the Holy Spirit where I am on what I call the ten-point scale of repentance. Am I closer to zero than I am to ten?"

"What happens after you have heard from the Holy Spirit?" I asked.

"The answer I get will determine whether I need to make adjustments, so that my life is actually producing fruits in accordance with my repentance."

"Sounds like I need to allow the Holy Spirit to examine my life as well," I said.

"Yes," said Stan, "and we should both take seriously what He has to say. Then comes the obedience. That will move our lives toward the right end of the scale: as close to ten as possible this side of eternity!"

Bible verses to consider:
Therefore bring forth fruits in keeping with your repentance. Luke 3:8.

Therefore if any man is in Christ, he is a new creature; the old things passed away; behold new things have come. 2 Corinthians 5:17.

Prayer: Thank you, Father, for speaking to me through your word and through the Holy Spirit. Thank you for providing the way for me to come before you in confession and repentance. I confess that what I do and say is often not in keeping with what you want through my repentance. Forgive me, and help me follow your lead in truly repenting, so that my life and everything in it brings forth fruits that are in keeping with my repentance. Thank you I can and do bring these prayers before you in the name of Jesus. Amen.

Think on this: Confession is one thing; repentance is another. If a person confesses sin but doesn't change anything, is that true confession? Who leads repentance? Is it you or is it God? Have you ever found yourself confessing to the same thing over and over because there has been no repentance? If so, what can be done about that? Can you do it on your own?

DAY 62

The How and What of Effective Prayers

"Near the end of James' letter," Stan began, "there's a verse about prayer that probably has resulted in countless books, classes, and discussions."

"Which verse is that?" I asked.

"'The effective prayer of a righteous person can accomplish much.'"

"A great promise," I said. "I suppose the questions are, 'What is effective prayer, and who is righteous enough?"

"Let's talk about the effective part today. Maybe later we can get to the part about who is righteous."

"Sounds good," I said. "So there's been a lot of discussions and writing on effective prayer?

"I imagine so. People trying to figure out the best way to pray. Methodology and the like. People thinking that if they just do it a little differently, maybe it will be more effective."

"I know I've wondered about that," I said. "Where do I pray? Do I sit, stand, or kneel? What do I say? What order do I say it? Sometimes I overthink it."

"I know," said Stan sympathetically. "The methodology part sure can be a trap that covers up the important part."

"Which is?"

"The 'accomplish much' part."

"Like moving the whole world with effective prayer?" I asked.

"I don't think so," Stan replied. "To me, the focus is to be on effective prayer accomplishing much in me."

"In what way?"

"I think the bottom-line purpose of prayer isn't to get whatever I want from God. He already knows my mind and heart. No, I think the reason God wants me to come before Him in prayer is so I can discover what's on His mind and heart."

"There's nothing I can tell Him that He doesn't already know," I agreed.

"That's right. What He wants is for me to know Him more deeply. And when that happens from my prayers," Stan added, "I think that's the 'much' James says we accomplish. If knowing God more intimately results from my prayers, what could possibly be more effective?"

"Seems to me," I replied, "our prayers can't be more effective than accomplishing that!"

"That's right. If those prayers result in changes in me that align more closely with what God intends for me to be and do, then they will indeed be effective."

"So instead of worrying about method," I said, "I just need to focus on what is to be accomplished: changing me!"

Bible verses to consider:
The effective prayer of a righteous man can accomplish much. James 5:16.

Hear, LORD, when I cry with my voice, and be gracious to me and answer me. When You said, "Seek My face," my heart said to You, "I shall seek Your face, LORD." Psalm 27:7-8.

Prayer: Thank you, Father, for allowing me to come before you in prayer. Thank you for wanting me to know what is on your mind and heart. I confess that too often I merely tell you what is on my mind and heart, when you already know everything. Please, Father, forgive me for those selfish and self-centered prayers. And please lead me in only seeking to know you better, so that my prayers are truly effective in accomplishing much. Draw me ever closer to you in a constantly deepening relationship. Thank you I can and do bring these prayers before you in the name of Jesus. Amen.

Think on this: Would you say your prayers are effective? Why or why not? How would you teach others to pray more effectively? Do your prayers tend to focus on telling God things that He already knows? Do you truly want to know what is on God's heart and mind? If that is what you want, how can it happen? What would you like God to accomplish in your relationship with Him?

DAY 63

Ready, Set, and Keep Going

"Do you remember when I shared how I used to have difficulty spending consistent time with God?" Stan asked.

"I do remember," I replied, "and I appreciated your honesty. You indicated it was nearly impossible for you."

"Starting was easy," Stan said. "I started and failed many times, probably more than I could count. But through God's grace, I was finally able to maintain having a time with God every day. A time of worship, devotion, reflection, and prayer."

"Every day?" I asked.

"Every day," he said. "And it's a time of real richness for me. I pray it will be the same for you, my friend, as well as for each person who calls on the name of the Lord."

"Thank you for praying for me," I said.

"Glad to. I was reminded of this whole subject this morning, while reading from Paul's second letter to his friend Timothy."

"What was the reminder?"

"Paul encouraged Timothy to complete what he had begun. While Paul was writing specifically about Timothy's ministry in the city of Ephesus (which was in modern day Turkey, by the way), I think it has application to whatever God encourages me to do. As I said, beginning something for God is easy."

"But continuing and completing is the hard part," I said.

"Sure is. And what do you think makes it so hard?" Stan asked.

"Well, as you often say," I replied, "Self, the world, the flesh, and the devil."

Stan nodded. "Focusing on what I want to do apart from God, rather than following His lead in being who He has for me to be. And that applies to something else we talk about all of the time."

"Do you mean discipleship?" I asked. "Is completing what God has for us another way to describe discipleship?"

"I think that's a good way to put it, my friend," Stan replied. "Just about everything in my relationship with God revolves around those same three steps of discipleship. A friend of mine calls it the 'Jesus Three Step'."

"The Jesus Three Step?"

"That's right. Step one, get me out of God's way. Step two, do what God has for me to do. Step three, follow Him wherever He leads, whatever the direction and whatever the cost."

"I'm glad you explained that," I replied with a smile. "There for a minute I was afraid we were going to start a dancing lesson. But seriously," I added, "I appreciate the reminder to follow God's lead."

Bible verses to consider:
Fulfill your ministry. 2 Timothy 4:5.

I have fought the good fight, I have finished the course, I have kept the faith; in the future there is laid up for me the crown of righteousness, which the Lord, the righteous Judge, will award to me on that day; and not only to me, but also to all who have loved His appearing. 2 Timothy 4:7-8.

And let endurance have its perfect result, so that you may be perfect and complete, lacking in nothing. James 1:4.

Prayer: Thank you, Father, that you want to have an ever-deepening relationship with me. Thank you that you not only led me to begin, but you encourage me to continue on with what you began. I confess I often fail to follow through with what you show me to do. Please forgive me and help me follow your lead so I will complete all you have for me to complete. Thank you I can and do bring these prayers before you in the name of Jesus. Amen.

Think on this: Have you been able to establish a regular time with God each day? If yes, how was that accomplished? Do you sense that your relationship with God is deepening? If you do not have a regular time with God, what changes can you make? How would those changes help you in the steps of discipleship?

DAY 64

He's Just Waiting

"After Jesus was baptized by John the Baptist," Stan began, "Luke says Jesus was led about in the wilderness by the Holy Spirit."

"Is that where Jesus was tempted by Satan?" I asked.

"That's right. And the whole account of that temptation is a valuable lesson for you and me, especially the last part."

"What's the last part?"

"When Satan finished with his every temptation, Luke says he departed from Jesus, but would be back at an 'opportune time'."

"An 'opportune time' sounds pretty ominous," I said.

"It is," Stan replied. "And that's an essential thing to know. Even though it may seem like Satan has decided to leave me alone when I'm able to resist his temptation, he's just waiting."

"For that opportune time. In other words," I said, "Satan hasn't decided to leave you alone, just because you've successfully resisted him?"

"Not on this side of eternity. He's just waiting for the right time to raise his ugly head and tempt me again. If I'm not aware that he's waiting," Stan added, "and if I don't call upon the Holy Spirit for constant help, I'm apt to fall into Satan's trap when he pounces."

"What might an opportune time look like?" I asked.

"Whenever and by whatever means Satan chooses," Stan replied.

"Do you think Satan is just waiting to take away your salvation?" I asked.

"Absolutely not," Stan replied. "Satan's temptations do not put me in danger of losing my salvation. That's been settled for all time by my acceptance of Christ's finished work on the cross. And Satan knows that. But he still tries to disrupt my testimony and, thereby, lead others astray."

"I certainly don't want to be part of that," I said.

"Neither do I," said Stan. "So let's both try to keep in mind that Satan is just waiting."

Bible verses to consider:
And when the devil had finished every temptation, he departed from Him until an opportune time. Luke 4:13.

If you do well, will not your countenance be lifted up? And if you do not do well, sin is crouching at the door; and its desire is for you, but you must master it. Genesis 4:7.

No temptation has overtaken you but such as is common to man; and God is faithful, who will not allow you to be tempted beyond what you are able, but with the temptation will provide the way of escape also, that you may be able to endure it. 1 Corinthians 10:13.

Submit therefore to God. Resist the devil and he will flee from you. James 4:7

Prayer: Thank you, Father, that you provide all I need to resist Satan's every temptation. Thank you for the knowledge that he waits for an opportune time to tempt me again. Please help me stay aware that Satan has not gone away, but is just waiting at the door of my life, to cause me to sin and to disrupt my testimony. I confess that too many times I have fallen into his trap. Please forgive me. Keep me alert, Father, to temptations that come at Satan's opportune times. Thank you I can and do bring these prayers before you in the name of Jesus. Amen.

Think on this: Do you believe that Satan wants to pull us down into his domain? How does he try to do that? How can you become more aware that Satan is waiting for an opportune time to tempt you? Do you think there is a way to prevent this? Why or why not? What may keep us from resisting his schemes? What would it look like for you to avail yourself of all that is available for such resistance?

DAY 65

Letting Him Do What He Came to Do

"A couple days ago," Stan began, "I noticed a plumber's truck at a neighbor's house. And yesterday, another came, from one of those companies that clean up water damage."

"What was that all about?" I asked.

"I found out when I went over to see if I could help in any way. Seems my neighbor noticed his hot water heater was leaking a little bit. He called the plumber to have a look, but they both got sidetracked. Turns out he had the plumber fix a couple other things, a faucet and a water pressure valve, but the plumber never got around to the hot water heater before it was time to leave for the day. In the middle of the night, it broke completely; the bottom fell out, and the basement was flooded. That's why the water damage people were there."

"That's a shame," I responded. "Probably a sure bet your neighbor wishes he'd had the plumber do what he called him for."

"You're right about that," Stan said, "and it's a lesson for my faith walk with God."

"How so?" I asked.

"The apostle John zeroed in on this in his first letter, where he makes a simple statement about why Jesus appeared on the earth."

"Which was what?"

"To destroy the works of the devil," said Stan. "I chose to have Jesus as an integral part of my life when I accepted His finished work on the cross. I got a new life through His resurrection, and received the indwelling Holy

Spirit, whom He asked His Father to send. So everything is in place to do what needs to be done. I just need to surrender to God so the works of Satan are destroyed in my life."

"And is that type of surrender just a matter of choosing it?"

"It is," Stan replied. "Choosing and keep choosing! The Bible's book of Revelation tells me that Satan's full and final destruction will occur one day. However, in the meantime, for as long as God keeps me on this side of eternity, I've got some choices to make. Jesus came to destroy the works of Satan, and I need to let Him do what He came to do. If I don't," Stan concluded, "like my neighbor's house, there may be a mess that needs to be cleaned up!"

Bible verses to consider:
The Son of God appeared for this purpose, that He might destroy the works of the devil. 1 John 3:8.

For the Son of Man has come to seek and to save that which was lost. Luke 19:10.

Prayer: Thank you, Father, for sending your Son into the world to destroy the works of Satan through His finished work on the cross, His death, and His resurrection. Thank you for those who brought me to the truth of your provision. Thank you, too, for the Holy Spirit who helps, counsels, and guides me to choose to have the works of Satan destroyed in my life. I confess that too often I do not choose to have those works destroyed. Please forgive me and help me surrender completely to all the Holy Spirit has for me, as I choose to accept His power to overcome the enemy. Thank you I can and do bring these prayers before you in the name of Jesus. Amen.

Think on this: It's easy to get sidetracked in just about everything, which distracts us from doing what needs to get done. The same applies to our faith walk. Jesus came to destroy the works of the devil, but the devil is persistent. Who are you going to follow? Are you consistent in letting Jesus do what He came to do? What would it look like to be more consistent? How can that be done?

DAY 66

Presenting the Truth in Different Ways

"I did one of my favorites things yesterday," I said to Stan one morning.

"What's that?" he asked.

"I spent time at the Big Barn Bookstore just wandering around," I replied. "I just love looking at books."

"See anything good?"

"Lots," I said, "but I was particularly struck by the number of Bibles and Christian books on the shelves. I was really surprised by how many there are."

"And you probably didn't see the half of it," Stan said.

"Why are there so many?" I replied. "Why so many different versions of the Bible? Why so many different books on different subjects about Christianity?"

"You ever had trouble understanding something the first time you heard or read it?" Stan asked.

"Of course," I replied.

"Me, too," Stan said. "I think one of the reasons it took me so long to become a Christian is that I needed to hear the same message in different words, before I could understand. Jesus often spoke in parables to different people. The truth wasn't any different; it was just presented in different ways to help them understand."

"So," I replied, "lots of different Bible versions and books on Christianity so people have a better chance of understanding. Is that what you're saying?"

"That's about it," Stan said. "As well, I think John's gospel records Jesus saying something that's on point."

"What's that?" I asked.

"It's near the end of the twelfth chapter," Stan replied, "where Jesus said Father God had told him what to say and what to speak. I think Jesus was making a distinction."

"You mean between 'saying' and 'speaking'?"

"Yes, Stan replied. "To me, Jesus seems to imply that the Father had told Him what to say: the truth. And He was to speak that truth in whatever way necessary to help the people understand it."

Bible verses to consider:
For I did not speak on my own initiative, but the Father Himself who sent Me has given Me commandment, what to say and what to speak. John 12:49.

Therefore I speak to them in parables; because while seeing they do not see, and while hearing they do not hear, nor do they understand. Matthew 13:13.

Prayer: Thank you, Father, for the truth of who you are, and of your gracious and free gift of salvation through the finished work of Jesus on the cross. Thank you for those who presented the truth to me in different ways, so I could finally understand, accept, and embrace it. Thank you for that truth: that Jesus has enabled me to know you ever more deeply on this side of eternity, and that through Him you have provided life eternally with you when it is time. Please help me follow your lead in presenting the truth in whatever way you know is appropriate for each person you bring before me. Thank you I can and do bring these prayers before you in the name of Jesus. Amen.

Think on this: The truth is the truth. Do you think the truth of the gospel should be presented in different ways? Why or why not? Is it okay for people to be creative in presenting the truth? Have you given thought to different ways you yourself might present it, whether speaking or writing? Is there someone in your life who may need to hear the truth in a different way, to understand? Are you willing to be used that way? If so, what might that look like?

DAY 67

Climbing Sycamore Trees

"I don't know much about trees," said Stan, "and I probably wouldn't recognize a sycamore if I saw one. But there's one mentioned in Luke's gospel that's really important to me."

"Luke wrote about sycamore trees?" I asked.

"Just one," Stan replied, "because a fellow had to climb it to see Jesus."

"Someone climbed a tree to see Him? What was that all about?"

"Jesus was passing through Jericho on His way to Jerusalem," Stan said, "and there was a man by the name of Zaccheus who wanted to see Jesus. Luke says he wasn't very tall and couldn't see over the crowd. So he climbed a sycamore tree as Jesus passed by."

"And that's important to you?" I asked.

"Sure is," Stan replied. "I didn't actually climb a tree, but I did have to adjust my life in order to see Jesus. This Zaccheus fellow realized he couldn't see Jesus from where he stood. Likewise, when God awakened in me the desire to know Him through Jesus, I realized I couldn't see Jesus without making adjustments in my life."

"What kind of adjustments?" I asked.

"I couldn't remain in the crowd where I was," Stan replied. "I needed to get somewhere else. I needed to 'climb a sycamore tree,' whatever it was, in order to get a clearer view of the Lord."

"Did you only have to do that once?"

"Once in terms of my eternal destination," Stan replied. "But there are sycamore trees all around me, meaning I need to reposition myself continually if I'm going to see Jesus and what He wants me to see on this side of eternity."

"Is this repositioning kind of like discipleship?" I asked.

"Not only 'kind of like,'" Stan replied. "I would say they are one and the same: doing whatever I need to do, in order to see Jesus clearly!

Bible verses to consider:
And He (Jesus) entered and was passing through Jericho. And behold, there was a man called by the name of Zaccheus; and he was a chief tax gatherer, and he was rich. And he was trying to see who Jesus was, and he was unable because of the crowd, for he was small in stature. And he ran on ahead and climbed up into a sycamore tree in order to see Him, for He was about to pass through that way. Luke 19:1-4.

Prayer: Thank you, Father, for wanting me to see you. Thank you for providing every way I need to see you and all you have for me on both sides of eternity. I confess I do not always make the effort required to see you. I do not choose to reposition myself, like Zaccheus climbing that tree, in order to see you. Please forgive me and help me follow your lead, whatever it is, so I can see you as clearly as possible. Thank you I can and do bring these prayers before you in the name of Jesus. Amen.

Think on this: Are there "sycamore trees" you need to climb in order to see Jesus more clearly? Do you need to get away from the crowd in order to climb those trees? If yes, what would it look like to get away from that crowd? If a particular tree seems too big for you to climb by yourself, how do you get the help you need?

DAY 68

Staying on the Altar

"I remember clearly," Stan began, "a morning service when I first became a Christian. The pastor, who was a bit of a character, was talking about being a living sacrifice. I didn't really understand what that meant, but I did get the joke the pastor told."

"What was the joke?" I asked.

"He said his problem with being a living sacrifice was he kept getting off the altar."

"Getting off the altar?"

"Yes," Stan said. "And the fact that I still remember His words from so long ago shows me the importance of what he said."

"What brought those words to mind?"

"This morning I was in Paul's letter to the Romans," Stan said, "and he was writing about being a living sacrifice. It struck me as if Paul had written it specifically to me."

"In what way?" I asked.

"I only have the opportunity to be a living sacrifice on this side of eternity," Stan said.

"So?"

"As far as I know, when my time of growing here is finished," he said, "and I get on the train, I will no longer have the opportunity to be a living sacrifice. So it's vital for me to examine how I'm spending the time I have remaining. Am I being the living sacrifice Paul wrote about? The living sacrifice God intends me to be?"

"How is a person supposed to do that?" I asked.

"For me," Stan replied, "it means I'm to stay on the altar as a living sacrifice, not go off in whatever direction I want apart from God. For me, crawling off is easy. Staying on is the more difficult part and can happen only as I surrender to the leading of the Holy Spirit. Every moment I am not who and what God intends by His salvation, my conversion, His sanctification and transformation, I am missing important opportunities to serve Him."

"Being a living sacrifice sounds a lot like being a disciple," I said.

"In what way?" Stan asked.

"Denying myself and doing what God has for me by taking up my cross while I follow wherever He leads."

"You're right, my friend," Stan said. "It does sound like being a disciple!"

Bible verse to consider:
I urge you therefore, brethren, by the mercies of God, to present your bodies a living and holy sacrifice, acceptable to God, which is your spiritual service of worship. Romans 12:1.

Prayer: Thank you, Father, for wanting me to be a living and holy sacrifice acceptable to you. Thank you, too, for providing the Holy Spirit to guide me in that sacrifice. I confess there have been way too many times where I have, in essence, crawled off the altar by refusing to be the living sacrifice you intend. Please forgive me. And please, Father, open me to see what you have for me to be and do as yours on this side of eternity, before my time of growing here is finished. Thank you I can and do bring these prayers before you in the name of Jesus. Amen.

Think on this: By definition, a person has to live for God in order to be a living sacrifice. Do you agree with that? Why or why not? What does it look like to be a living sacrifice? Is that what you look like? Why or why not? How does a person keep from crawling off the altar and going in a direction different from what God intends? What can help a person be the living sacrifice God intends?

DAY 69

Getting Out of the Way

"Last weekend," Stan began, "my wife and I drove out towards Grangerville. We wanted to pick up some of those fabulous blueberries the farmers grow out there."

"Get some?" I asked.

"Yeah, finally," Stan replied. "But it took just about forever to get there!"

"Was there a problem?" I asked.

"Well, I should know better," Stan responded, "but farm folks don't drive as fast as city dwellers. And they have stuff to move down the road that sometimes gets in the way of those wanting to go faster."

"What kind of stuff?" I asked.

"Tractors, trailers, all kinds of things," Stan replied.

"Is that what happened with you?" I asked.

"It is," Stan replied. "We got behind a farmer and his tractor on a narrow road, and I just couldn't get by. He finally came to a wide spot and pulled over to let us pass."

"That was nice of him," I said.

"It was," Stan replied, "and it showed me a real lesson for my faith walk."

"How did a farmer and his tractor on a country road show you a spiritual lesson?"

"Well," he said, "as I thought about it later, I had the picture of me driving the slow tractor down the road of life. The Holy Spirit is waiting patiently for me to pull over and get out of His way. Way too often I'm just chugging along, going at my own pace, doing what I want to do, heading in whatever direction I want. But the Holy Spirit wants me to get out of His way so He can be in front."

"Kind of hard to follow if you're in the front," I said.

"Exactly!" Stan replied. "And though it can take me way too long, it's best when I glance over my shoulder, see the Holy Spirit, and pull over out of His way. Then He can lead, with me following."

"Does the Holy Spirt then zoom off, leaving you behind?" I asked.

"Nope," Stan replied. "He's in front leading, going at a pace He knows I can follow. But every once in a while He will look over His shoulder and ask if I'm ready to speed up a little!"

Bible verses to consider:
And I will ask the Father, and He will give you another Helper, that He may live with you forever; that is the Spirit of truth, whom the world cannot receive, because it does not behold Him or know Him, but you know Him because He abides with you and will be in you. John 14:16-17.

If we live by the Spirit, let us also walk by the Spirit. Galatians 5:25.

Follow me. John 21:19.

Prayer: Thank you, Father, for wanting to lead me in every aspect of my life. Thank you, too, for wanting me to get out of your way so you can lead. I confess that way too often I fail to yield to what you want, and I fail to get myself out of your way so you can lead. Please forgive me. I ask you to move in me according to your will, so I will choose to get out of your way, letting you lead as I follow. Thank you I can and do bring all of these prayers before you in the name of Jesus. Amen.

Think on this: Are there areas in your life where you need to pull over and let the Holy Spirit get by so He can lead? If so, would you like to get out of His way? Why or why not? If you want to get out of the Holy Spirit's way, what will it take for that to happen? Is that something you want? Why or why not? How is getting out of the Holy Spirit's way related to the steps of discipleship: denying self, taking up your cross, and following?

DAY 70

Can't Be Taught Without Being Teachable

"One of my neighbors is a teacher at Brown's Middle School," said Stan. "She and her husband were over for dinner last night."

"Nice time?" I asked.

"Very," Stan replied. "Great people and wonderful neighbors."

"What does she teach?"

"A couple of subjects, but history is her specialty. I've heard she's a very good teacher. Last night we were talking about how she engages her students in wanting to learn. Without engaging them, there's not a whole lot a teacher can do. So she spends a lot of time building into the students the desire to learn."

"The love of learning?" I replied.

"That's it," Stan said. "Without that desire it's hard, maybe impossible, to teach. But with it, there is virtually no limit to what a student can learn. Not unlike our relationship with God."

"How so?" I asked.

"Well," Stan replied, "I've seen it with a lot of people. I saw it with me. I said I wanted a closer relationship with God, but I didn't do anything about it. I just didn't have the motivation to have a closer relationship with God."

"And as you often say, eternal life is about knowing God the Father and Jesus the Son," I said. "If a person doesn't have the desire to know them, it might not happen."

"More than might," Stan replied. "I would say that it won't happen. As for myself, the person I know best, I used to spend a lot of time praying that God would teach me, but any such desire to be taught ended with my prayer."

"Ended with your prayer?" I replied. "But something must have changed at some point. What was it?"

"One day I was praying, asking God to fill me with all He had for me," Stan said, "and all of a sudden I had this sense of God replying in a new way."

"What was that?" I asked.

"God's response was something like this: He'd heard that prayer from me many times, but He didn't see that I'd done anything to prepare for what I was asking."

"What did you think that meant?" I asked.

"Bottom-line," Stan replied, "is that God made it clear I wasn't teachable. I had asked Him to fill me with all He had for me, but I hadn't made any room for Him. I was still full of the stuff that kept out what God wanted to pour in. To show I was teachable and truly desired God to change me, I needed to make room for Him. I had to choose to be emptied."

"Again, this seems like the first step in discipleship: denying self."

"That's it, my friend," Stan replied. "I needed to deny myself the things apart from God that were filling my life. Until I did that, I couldn't proceed into a deeper relationship of knowing the Father and the Son."

Bible verses to consider:

Teach me Thy way, O Lord; I will walk in Thy truth; unite my heart to fear Thy name. Psalm 86:11.

Lead me in Thy truth and teach me, for Thou art the God of my salvation; for Thee I wait all the day. Psalm 25:5.

But seek first His kingdom and His righteousness; and all these things shall be added to you. Matthew 6:33.

Jesus therefore answered them, and said, "My teaching is not Mine, but His who sent Me." John 7:16.

Prayer: Thank you, Father, for wanting to teach me all there is to know about you, the Son and the Holy Spirit. I confess that too often I am not teachable, because I choose other things and other ways rather than yours. Please forgive that foolishness, and help me follow each step of your lead as you seek to teach me. Please, Father, help me to be open to being teachable in accordance with what you want and have for me. Thank you I can and do bring these prayers before you in the name of Jesus. Amen.

Think on this: Do you think you are teachable? Do you want to learn all that God has for you? If no, what might be in the way of your learning? Do you want to know God and what He has for you? Why or why not? What would it look like for you to be teachable just as God wants? Is that something you want? If so, do you know how it can happen?

DAY 71

You Can't Earn It

"We had dinner at the Good Fortune Chinese Restaurant again last night," Stan said.

"One of my favorites." I replied. "How was it?"

"Food was wonderful, service was great, and the fortune cookie tasted just fine," Stan replied. "But the fortune in the cookie was wrong."

"Wrong?" I said. "How could a fortune in a cookie be wrong?"

"Bad information and bad advice," Stan said.

"What was so bad?"

"It said, 'Everything you desire must be earned.'"

"Oh," I said, "I see what you mean. Certainly bad information and advice when it comes to spending eternity with God when it's time."

"And I'm really glad the fortune is wrong!" said Stan. "I hate to think how much work would be involved in trying to earn my way into God's eternal presence."

"It's impossible to earn God's favor on my own, right?" I asked.

"Yes, and trying would be a lot of work for nothing."

"But aren't there people really desiring to be in God's eternal presence and trying to earn it?"

"Yes. Sadly, they don't know that salvation is God's gift, gracious and free and accepted by faith. For whatever reason, they are blinded to that truth and locked in the bondage of working for God's favor. It can't be earned, but they keep trying."

"How can such people be released from that bondage?" I asked.

"By knowing and accepting what Jesus accomplished by His life, death, and resurrection."

"How are they going to know that?" I asked.

"It will happen," Stan said, "if those of us who know the truth are committed to sharing that truth with those who don't know."

Bible verses to consider:
For by grace you have been saved through faith; and that not of yourselves, it is the gift of God; not as a result of works, that no one should boast. Ephesians 2:8-9.

How then shall they call upon Him in whom they have not believed? And how shall they believe in Him they have not heard? Romans 10:14.

Jesus therefore was saying to those Jews who had believed in Him, "If you abide in My word, then you are truly disciples of Mine; and you shall know the truth, and the truth shall set you free." John 8:31-32.

When Jesus therefore had received the sour wine, He said, "It is finished!" And He bowed His head, and gave up His spirit. John 19:30.

Prayer: Thank you, Father, for your free and gracious gift of salvation through the finished work of Jesus on the cross. Thank you I can look forward to spending eternity with you when it's time, because I have accepted your free gift through faith. Thank you that I don't have to work my way to heaven. I pray for those who want to be in your eternal presence when it's time, but who think they have to work their way there. I pray for each one to be freed by your grace and the truth of free salvation. Please help me follow every step of your lead, so I can help others know the truth. Thank you I can and do bring these prayers before you in the name of Jesus. Amen.

Think on this: Do you know you can't work your way to heaven? Have you accepted the free and gracious gift of eternal salvation? If no, why? Do you know people who are in the bondage of trying very hard to work their way into heaven? How can you share the truth with them? If you have been freed by the truth, are you doing all you can to help others be free also? If no, why? What would it look like for you to be doing that? Can you see yourself in that role? Why or why not?

DAY 72

What's Your "Rather Be?"

"You ever notice those bumper stickers and license plate holders that say something like, 'I'd rather be' someplace else, doing something else?"

"Sure have," I replied. "Just saw two on the way here this morning. One said the person would rather be in Hawaii. The other said, 'I'd rather be sailing.' Maybe if they got together, they would be sailing in Hawaii!"

"Yeah," Stan said, "it seems like a lot of people wish they weren't where they are."

"How about you, Stan?" I responded. "Wish you were somewhere else doing something different?"

"Yes and no," he said.

"How can it be both?" I asked.

"In the first place," he said, "I'm very much looking forward to being in God's eternal presence, so, yes, I wish I was there. On the other hand, I'm content to be where God has me, doing what He's given me to do now. So no, there's no place I'd rather be than where God presently has me."

"Have you always been that content?"

"Well, in my pre-Christian days–and I think this was part of God's plan for me–I became increasingly discontent with where I was in my relationship with God."

"Where were you in that?" I asked.

"Nowhere," he said. "And that was the problem. I simply didn't have any relationship with Him. He was not part of my life. However, through

His grace and mercy, He gave me the desire to be somewhere else: closer to Him."

"Okay," I replied, "that was pre-Christian. What about today?"

"As I said," Stan responded, "if I don't watch my heart, there's always the tendency to wish I was someplace else doing something else."

"And how do you avoid that?" I asked.

"Surrender," was Stan's one-word response. "Surrender to the Holy Spirit, who is in me for the very purpose of leading me in an ever-deepening faith walk. If I will accept where God has for me to be, doing what He has for me to do, I won't be discontent, looking to be somewhere else."

"So," I said, "it's kind of like driving around with a bumper sticker that says, 'I'd rather be walking closer to God.'"

"Exactly," Stan replied, "and it can't just be wishful thinking!"

Bible verses to consider:
For a day in Thy courts is better than a thousand outside. I would rather stand at the threshold of the house of my God, than dwell in the tents of the wicked. Psalm 84:10.

Not that I speak from want; for I have learned to be content in whatever circumstances I am in. Philippians 4:11.

Prayer: Thank you, Father, for the contentment you provide, in knowing I will spend eternity in your presence. Thank you, too, for the contentment found in drawing ever closer to you in a personal relationship. I know that the desire to be someplace else is from the world, the flesh, and the devil. Please, Father, help me resist the temptation when my thoughts and desires take me away from your will. Please help me so that my "I'd rather be" is only closer to you. Thank you I can and do bring these prayers before you in the name of Jesus. Amen.

Think on this: We all think about places we would rather be, such as building sand castles on a Hawaiian beach rather than shoveling snow in

Colorado, or lounging in bed rather than going to work. What are some of your own "rather be's?" How about being closer to God rather than closer to the world, the flesh, and the devil? Is that something you would like? If so, do you know how it can happen?

DAY 73

A Boatload of Lessons

"This morning," said Stan, "I was reading and journaling about Matthew's account of Peter walking on water. You remember that story?"

"We've talked some about it," I replied, "but fill me in on what you're learning."

"You'll recall it was right after the miracle where Jesus fed the five thousand with just a little bit of food," Stan said. "He told the disciples to get in the boat and go ahead to the other side of the Sea of Galilee. They obeyed but didn't know a storm was brewing. After spending time with His Father in prayer, Jesus headed towards the disciples."

"And He wasn't in a boat, right?" I said.

"No. He walked on the water to where the disciples were struggling against the storm. They couldn't believe their eyes when they saw Him. That's when Jesus told Peter to get out of the boat and walk on the water with Him."

"That's really amazing," I said.

"It is, and even though we have talked a little about this before, it's important and good for us to review what it teaches us each day."

"You've said before that the story applies to wherever we find ourselves," I recalled.

"That's right. And sometimes God may want us to be somewhere else. And then there's what Jesus said to Peter: 'Come.' And Peter heard Him."

"And you're good at reminding me that I need to have my spiritual ears open so I can hear God's voice."

"Right again. If I'm in a situation where I can't hear what God is saying, I'm going to miss out."

"Miss out on what?" I asked.

"Whatever God is trying to say to me," Stan replied.

"Okay," I responded, "Peter heard Jesus say 'Come.' What next?"

"Peter got out of the boat," Stan replied. "And that's a crucial lesson worth repeating. If I don't choose to move myself out of whatever situation I'm in, there's little chance God will do what He wants to do. While I know He can do whatever He wants, I can't expect Him to grab me and pull me out of my 'boat.' He wants me to choose to get out."

"And then Peter walked on the water, right?"

"Yes, and the direction he walked is the next lesson for us."

"Towards Jesus," I said.

"Right again. And we need to do the same. If I leave the circumstances God calls me to leave, but I don't go towards Him, I'll miss the wonderful opportunity of walking with Him wherever He wants to lead."

Bible verses to consider:
And He said, "Come!" And Peter got out of the boat, and walked on the water and came toward Jesus. Matthew 14:29.

If anyone wishes to come after Me, let him deny himself, and take up his cross daily, and follow Me. Luke 9:23.

Prayer: Thank you, Father, for always wanting me to follow you. Thank you for showing me when I must leave a comfortable place, even though I may not necessarily want to leave. I confess I often fail to hear your voice or make any effort to follow you. Please forgive me and continue to lead me. I need and I ask for your help to follow every step of your lead. Thank you I can and do bring these prayers before you in the name of Jesus. Amen.

Think on this: What does the "boat" of your life look like? Are you comfortable in that boat? Why or why not? Has God ever called you to get out of that boat and do something you have never done before? If yes, what was that like? If He has not, do you want Him to? If you respond to His "Come!" how might you see changes in your life?

DAY 74

Do You Have that Sinking Feeling?

"Yesterday," said Stan, "we talked about Peter getting out of the boat to walk on the water."

"It's an amazing story," I said. "Makes me wonder what that would feel like."

"Me, too, Stan replied. "And there's another part of Peter's adventure that I'd like to talk about."

"Let's have it," I responded.

"I have no idea how long Peter was actually walking on the water," Stan replied. "But there's something about the story that matters more than that, something for my lifelong faith walk."

"What's that?" I asked.

"Peter came full circle in his faith," Stan replied.

"Full circle? What's that mean?"

"First, Peter got out of the boat and walked towards Jesus. That was a great demonstration of the kind of faith I need to have."

"Walk towards Jesus," I repeated.

"Yes, but then Peter took his eyes off Jesus and began looking at the wind. Bad move! I do the same thing all the time. I take my eyes off Jesus and look at whatever circumstances I'm facing in my life."

"I can sure relate to that," I replied. "It's way too easy to focus on some trouble in my circumstances before everything else."

"After Peter focused on the wind and waves, he became afraid and began to sink. He allowed his mind to focus on the trouble rather than on Jesus. He had greater fear of the circumstances than faith in Jesus."

"Been there, done that," I replied.

"Me, too," Stan said, "but what Peter did next is a great demonstration of closing the circle by coming back to faith."

"What did he do?"

"He cried out to Jesus," Stan replied. "Smart move, and a great practical approach for me in everything I face. I'm to keep my focus on Jesus, but if my focus wanders onto something else, and I get that sinking feeling that things aren't going the right way, I am to come full circle and return to Jesus."

Bible verses to consider:
But seeing the wind, he (Peter) became afraid, and beginning to sink, he cried out, saying "Lord, save me!" Matthew 14:30.

They cried out to the LORD in their trouble, and He brought them out of their distresses. He caused the storm to be still, so that the waves of the sea were hushed. Then they were glad because they were quiet, so He guided them to their desired harbor. Psalm 107:28-30.

Prayer: Thank you, Father, for the truth of scripture and the practical applications you have for my walk with you. I confess that too often I take my eyes off you, focusing on my circumstances and becoming afraid, rather than resting in the security of your arms. Please forgive me. And please, Father, lead me, and help me to follow, trusting you fully in my circumstances. Give me the wisdom to call out to you if I wander away. Thank you I can and do bring all these prayers before you in the name of Jesus. Amen.

Think on this: You ever have that sinking feeling that comes from taking your eyes off Jesus? If so, what was that like? What kind of circumstances can cause you to lose your focus on Jesus? How can you correct that? What would it look like to have your focus on Jesus all the time, regardless of your circumstances? Do you want that to happen? If so, do you know how?

DAY 75

Having or Being Breakfast

"A neighbor couple just came back from a trip to East Africa. They invited us over last night to see photos."

"Was it a missionary trip?" I asked.

"They did visit some Christian missionaries, but that wasn't their primary focus. They spent about half their time in cities, and the other half in the bush on safari."

"That's one of my dream vacations," I replied. "Have you ever been?"

"Not yet," Stan said, "but a safari is certainly high on the list of things I want to experience before I get on the train."

"Did your neighbors enjoy the trip?"

"Sure seems like they did. They came back with some fabulous pictures, stories, and memories. A real adventure. One of their stories reminded me of what I was reading in the apostle Peter's first letter."

"He didn't go to Africa, did he?"

"I don't think so," Stan replied, "but he did write about a roaring lion. At least that's how he described Satan. He said the devil prowls around seeking someone to devour. Our friends said that every morning in the bush, they'd get up early and head out with a guide. They said the animals were magnificent, but what the creatures did to one another was sometimes difficult to look at."

"In what way?"

"Some of the animals were either having breakfast, or they were being breakfast. The stronger adversary prevailed."

"Having or being breakfast," I repeated. "Interesting way to describe it."

"Peter described Satan that way," Stan continued, "and I want to make certain that I'm never devoured by Satan. He just loves to pull me down and make me an ineffective Christian. He may not literally consume me, but he can sure take a big bite out of my walk with God if I'm not constantly vigilant. I have to watch out for his prowling and his desire to devour. And I can say without a doubt that I vastly prefer sitting here with you, my friend, having breakfast rather than being breakfast for Satan and his minions."

"So how do you avoid being breakfast?" I asked.

"Peter described it as being alert," Stan said. "Be alert to what Satan wants to do; be alert through total and continual surrender to the watchful presence of the Holy Spirit. I have to know the Holy Spirit will guard me, as I choose to let Him do so."

Bible verses to consider:
Be of sober spirit, be on the alert. Your adversary, the devil, prowls about like a roaring lion, seeking someone to devour. 1 Peter 5:8.

No temptation has overtaken you but such as is common to man; and God is faithful, who will not allow you to be tempted beyond what you are able, but with the temptation will provide the way of escape also, that you may be able to endure it. 1 Corinthians 10:13.

Prayer: Thank you, Father, for providing the Holy Spirit to live in me, to help, counsel, and guide me. Thank you that He watches over me and protects me from Satan, who seeks to devour me and destroy my witness. I want only to be yours in everything. Please, Father, help me follow your lead, away from the devouring influence of the evil one. Thank you I can and do bring these prayers before you in the name of Jesus. Amen.

Think on this: Do you believe Satan wants to devour you? Why or why not? Have you ever sensed you were being devoured by Satan? If yes, what was that like? What does it mean to be on the alert for Satan's activity? What is the best way to stay alert? Do you know the way out of every temptation?

DAY 76

Who Is This?

"I was in Matthew's gospel again this morning," Stan said, "reading and journaling, and I saw an absolutely essential question for my faith walk."

"What's the question?" I asked.

"As Jesus entered Jerusalem, where He would soon face the cross, there was a large crowd going before Him. Matthew records that all the city was stirred to ask, 'Who is this?'"

"The whole city?"

"That's what it says. And that's the essential question that I, and each person, must ask about Jesus: who is this? And not only ask, but be open to the answer that changes everything. By learning the right answer, and accepting that answer, my own eternal destination changed forever."

"Is this a question that has to be asked and answered more than once?"

"Well," Stan replied, "for eternal purposes, it only takes one right answer. However, I can continually learn more about Jesus through considering variations of the question."

"What do you mean by variations?"

"I mean making the question even more pointed, such as, 'Who is this who wants me to deny myself? Who is this who wants me to take up my cross? Who is this who is seeking to lead me? Who is this who wants me to follow Him?'"

"That's a lot of questions," I said.

"Yes, but there's really only one right answer," Stan responded. "and it's the same for each: Jesus."

Bible verses to consider:
And when He had entered Jerusalem, all the city was stirred, saying, "Who is this?" Matthew 21:10.

And He said to them, "But who do you say that I am?" And Peter answered and said, "The Christ of God." Luke 9:20.

Prayer: Thank you, Father, for leading me to ask and accept the answer about Jesus. Thank you for showing me the answer so I am assured of my eternal destination with you forever when it's time. And thank you for showing me who you are and what you want for the rest of my time on this side of eternity. I confess I too often do not ask and do not want to hear what you have for me. Please forgive me. And please, Father, lead me exactly as you want. Help me to follow. Help me to know, "Who is this?" Thank you I can and do bring these prayers before you in the name of Jesus. Amen.

Think on this: Have you asked the vital question "Who is this?" regarding Jesus? If so, how did you answer? Do you have assurance of life eternally with God when it's time? How about for this side of eternity? How would you answer Stan's various "Who is this?" questions? If you are uncertain, do you know how to find the answer? What have you learned so far about Jesus in your faith walk? Why do you think it is important to find out who Jesus is?

DAY 77

Obedience: an Obligation or a Privilege?

"Do you think God needs your obedience?" Stan asked one morning.

"Yeah, I guess so," I said rather awkwardly. "Haven't thought much about it. What do you think?"

"I don't think God needs my obedience," he replied, "but whether He wants it is a whole different question. When God shows me something that requires my obedience, He doesn't force me to do anything. He leaves it up to me. I think obedience is a matter of free will. I can do what I want."

"Would God bother to give the opportunity to obey," I asked, "if He didn't want you to do it?"

"Probably not," Stan replied. "but when I choose not to obey, it's my loss, not God's."

"Your loss in what way?"

"I think I lose out in at least three ways. First, I lose the opportunity to be involved in what God is doing. Can you imagine purposefully choosing to miss out on joining God in His activity?"

"That sounds like a serious loss," I said.

"Definitely," said Stan. "Second, by choosing not to obey, I lose the opportunity to get to know God better. And as we've often talked about, Jesus said that knowing God is eternal life. Again, what a loss!"

"Okay," I replied, "that's two. What's the third loss?"

"Pleasing God," Stan said. "While God doesn't need my obedience, I'm convinced, beyond a shadow of doubt, that He sure is pleased when He offers me the opportunity to be obedient and I choose Him over everything that doesn't include Him. To not hear His 'Well done!' is a loss I never want to experience!"

"So," I responded, "considering all the potential losses from choosing not to obey, would it be fair to say that obedience is a privilege, not an obligation?"

"Exactly," Stan replied. "I look at obedience to God as something I get to do, rather than something I have to do!"

Bible verses to consider:
If you love Me, you will keep My commandments. John 14:15.

He who has My commandments and keeps them, he it is who loves Me; and he who loves Me shall be loved by My Father, and I will love him, and will disclose Myself to him. John 14:21.

If you keep My commandments, you will abide in My love; just as I have kept My Father's commandments, and abide in His love. John 15:10.

Prayer: Thank you, Father, for giving me many opportunities to obey you. I confess there have been too many times I've chosen not to obey. Please forgive me. You know, and I know, that each time of failed obedience is my loss. I feel those losses, and I do not want them repeated. Please, Father, move in me so I follow you wherever you lead. Please help me draw ever closer to you in every step of my obedience. Thank you I can and do bring these prayers before you in the name of Jesus. Amen.

Think on this: Do you ever think about why you obey God? Or why you don't obey Him? Do you look on your obedience to God as a privilege? Why or why not? Do you look on obedience to God as an obligation? Why or why not? How does obeying God help you to know Him better?

DAY 78

The Reversible Jacket

"Nice jacket!" I said to Stan as I sat down. "New?"

"No," he replied, "I've had it for some time. It's reversible, so today I turned the inside out so it looks like a new jacket."

"Reversible jackets are a really great idea," I said. "Like having two for the price of one."

"More like two for the price of one and a half," Stan said with a smile. "You know, wearing a reversible jacket reminds me of what my faith walk with God is supposed to be about."

"In what way?" I asked.

"Transformation has to come from the inside out," Stan replied. "But unlike this jacket, I'm not supposed to keep reversing my life or behavior."

"Don't walk with God one way one day, then flip it the next–is that what you're saying?"

"Exactly," Stan replied. "Once God has begun the process of transformation, it is to continue. I shouldn't keep flip-flopping. He wants the process to take place in all parts of my life, not just some of them. I shouldn't wear His jacket of transformation for certain things, then turn it inside out for others."

"Kind of like wearing the jacket one way on Sundays," I said, "and then wearing it other side out during the week."

"That's right," Stan replied. "And even beyond Sunday, I'm not to wear it one way for certain things or with certain people, then turn it inside out in other situations. I've heard people describe that behavior as 'compartmentalizing' their faith. Manifesting being a Christian in some parts of their life, but not others."

"Is that very common?" I asked.

"Afraid so," Stan replied. "I've seen it in others, and I've seen it in myself."

"How can a person avoid that?"

"It's a choice," Stan said. "I have to be deliberate about my faith walk. I have to surrender myself to the Holy Spirit, and then choose to follow His lead."

"Sounds like discipleship," I replied.

"Right again, my friend," Stan said. "Denying myself means thinking of my life as a spiritually irreversible jacket: living for God every day, not reversing my life, but following wherever He wants to lead."

"Maybe reversible jackets aren't such a great idea after all," I replied.

"They serve a purpose," Stan said, "just not in my Christian life!"

Bible verses to consider:
But we all, with unveiled face beholding as in a mirror the glory of the Lord, are being transformed into the same image from glory to glory, just as from the Lord, the Spirit. 2 Corinthians 3:18.

And do not be conformed to this world, but be transformed by the renewing of your mind; that you may prove what the will of God is, that which is good and acceptable and perfect. Romans 12:2.

Prayer: Thank you, Father, for all you provide for me through the life, death, and resurrection of Jesus Christ. Thank you for your gracious and free gift of life eternally with you when my time here is done. Thank you, too, for the opportunity to pursue knowing you on this side of eternity. Thank you also for the presence of the Holy Spirit to counsel, guide, and help transform me into the image of Christ. I confess I often seek to look good on my own, rather than surrendering to the transformative power of the Holy Spirit. Forgive me for refusing to be changed from the inside out. Help me follow your lead, giving myself fully to be molded, shaped, and transformed by you. Thank you I can and do bring these prayers before you in the name of Jesus. Amen.

Think on this: Do you wear a "reversible jacket" in your relationship with God, depending on where you are and what you are doing? If so, Why? What does it look like for people to not compartmentalize their faith, being one way here and one way there? If you find yourself putting your faith into compartments, how can that be avoided. Do you agree that such compartmentalization may be too common in the church? Why or why not?

DAY 79

A Full-Time Disciple?

As Ricky came by to take our breakfast order, he asked, "Did you guys see the 'Help Wanted' sign in the window?"

We nodded, and Stan asked, "Is it a full-time position?"

"It is," Ricky replied. "If you know anyone looking for a job, please send him or her our way. We really need some help!"

"Will do," Stan said.

Ricky took our order, then hurried away.

"Full-time position," Stan said. "Just like being a disciple. That's what God is looking for: believers who are willing to be disciples all the time."

"Can a person be a part-time disciple?" I asked.

"While I think it's certainly possible," he said, "I also think that's not what God has in mind, or what Jesus was talking about when He told people about being disciples."

"Denying self, doing what He has for us to do, and following Him," I responded. "Full-time?"

"I think so," Stan replied. "Imagine if someone was hired here to be a full-time worker, but only showed up once in a while, for a few hours. That's not going to work out very well. Same with being a disciple. It's to be a full-time commitment."

"But what if a person doesn't have time to do that?" I asked.

"Time to be a disciple?" said Stan. "Note that Jesus put it in terms of 'being' not 'doing' discipleship. How could a person not have time to be a disciple?"

"But isn't being a disciple supposed to result in doing something?"

"Absolutely," Stan replied. "And that's the whole point. I first have to be a full-time disciple before I can find out what God has for me to do as I follow Jesus. And after I find out what He has for me to do, then comes the part about obeying what He has shown me."

Bible verses to consider:
If any one wishes to come after Me, let him deny himself, and take up his cross, and follow Me. For whoever wishes to save his own life shall lose it; but whoever loses his life for My sake shall find it. Matthew 16:24-25.

If anyone wishes to come after Me, let him deny himself, take up his cross daily, and follow Me. For whoever wishes to save his life shall lose it, but whoever loses his life for My sake, he is the one who will save it. Luke 9:23-24.

Prayer: Thank you, Father, for your provision of eternal salvation through the finished work of Jesus on the cross. Thank you, too, that you've called me to be a disciple for all the time remaining before I step into your eternal presence. Thank you that being a disciple is a full-time commitment, and that you will show me what you have for me to do for you and your kingdom. I confess that too often I do not listen to you, and even when I listen, I don't always obey. Forgive me and help me be the full-time disciple that you intend. Thank you I can and do bring these prayers before you in the name of Jesus. Amen.

Think on this: Do you agree that being a disciple is a full-time commitment? Why or why not? If you agree that it is full-time, how are you doing with that? What is the connection between "being" a disciple and "doing" what disciples do? If you sense you are not a full-time disciple, but would like to be one, do you know how that can happen?

DAY 80

First You Have to Get Up

"This morning I was looking at the account of the apostle Paul, who was then known as Saul, on his way to Damascus to persecute Christians," Stan said.

"Jesus interrupted his journey big time," I replied.

"Not only his journey, but his life and eternal destination. And I see a parallel between what Jesus said to him and what God says to me every single day."

"Do mean the part where He asked Saul, 'Why are you persecuting me?'"

"No," Stan replied, "it's what happened next."

"What was that?" I asked.

"Quick recap," Stan replied. "Saul was on his way to Damascus to bother the Christians; Jesus appeared like a flash of light from heaven; Saul was knocked to the ground; Jesus asked Saul why he was persecuting Him. After that comes the part I hear every morning: Jesus telling Saul to get up and go where Jesus wanted him to go, so Saul could find out what he was supposed to do."

"You hear that every morning?" I asked. "In what way?"

"Just like Saul had to get up off the ground to continue to Damascus," Stan replied, "God wakes me and says it's time to get up and go where He directs, so I can hear what He has to say. I'm to go to whatever 'Damascus' God has for me this side of heaven. Saul was told what to do there, and the same is true for me."

"And what's that?" I asked.

"The specifics are different each day," Stan replied, "but the goal is always the same: to continue my ever-deepening relationship with God. As I choose to follow Him, God leads and transforms me in accordance with His will."

"Kind of like working out the salvation that has been worked in?" I asked.

"Not just 'kind of like,'" Stan said. "Exactly like!"

"But the first step," I responded, "is for you to get up. Is that the point?"

"That's it," Stan replied. "For me, it's essential that I make the choice to move from where I am to my 'Damascus,' so I can be in the right place to hear what God has for me to do."

Bible verses to consider:
Rise and enter the city, and it shall be told you what you must do. Acts of the Apostles 9:6.

Work out your salvation with fear and trembling; for it is God who is at work in you, both to will and to work for His good pleasure. Philippians 2:12, 13.

Prayer: Thank you, Father, that you want to tell me what it is you have for me to do in response to your free and gracious provision of salvation. Thank you, too, for making it clear that I have to be where you want me to be in order to hear what you are saying. I confess that I often choose to be elsewhere. Please help me follow your lead to where you intend for me to be, doing what you want, wherever and whatever that may be. Thank you I can and do bring these prayers before you in the name of Jesus. Amen.

Think on this: Do you spend time with God each day to hear what He has to say to you? If not, what is keeping you from "getting up" to hear from Him? Do you think it's important to hear what God has for you to do? Why or why not? If you think it is important and you would like to have that sort of time with God, do you know how it can happen?

DAY 81

Walking Down Different Streets

"Do you remember when we talked about measuring where we are on the scale of repentance?" Stan asked.

I do," I said. "We talked about John the Baptist telling people they need to live in ways that show their repentance—and the same is true for us today."

"Exactly," Stan replied. "And last night God showed me something similar, from a different perspective. I was glad He enabled me to have my spiritual eyes open to see it."

"What did He show you?"

"I was looking in a book that I hadn't pulled off the shelf for a long time. There was a piece of paper in it that I'd used to mark my place. It was a photocopy I don't even remember making."

"What was it?" I asked.

"A little story written by a woman named Portia Nelson; while it didn't use the word 'repentance,' it had a lesson for progressing in it."

"Progressing?" I replied. "A person can progress with repentance?"

"Absolutely!" Stan exclaimed. "Much of our repentance is like taking two steps forward and one step back–making progress, but sometimes slipping. The story I copied was about walking down a street. A woman fell in a hole and took seemingly forever to find a way out. The next day she walked down the same street, fell into the same hole, and again took a long time getting out. The third day, she fell into the same hole, but got right out."

"How did the story end?"

"She walked down that street, saw the same hole, and this time walked around it. But finally, she started walking down a different street."

"Lots of wisdom in a few words," I said.

"You've got that right, my friend. That little story has a valuable lesson about repentance. If I say I'm not going to continue doing such and such, but I refuse to accept the help of the Holy Spirit, I will just continue falling into the same old problems, failures or sins."

"That's something I do all the time," I responded. "And I really get tired of it!"

"Tired enough to change?" Stan asked. "That's a question the Holy Spirit keeps asking me. If I listen and follow, I'll truly repent and avoid the route with the pits and falls. It's real easy to condemn myself for failed repentance. But it's essential not to end my efforts even if I fail again and again. I'm to measure my progress listening and following the Holy Spirit. If I do that, there will come a time I can look back and rejoice because I'm walking down God's street, not the streets of self, the world, the flesh, and the devil!"

Bible verses to consider:
Repent and turn to God, performing deeds appropriate to repentance. Acts of the Apostles 26:20.

Therefore bring forth fruits in keeping with your repentance. Luke 3:8.

I can do all things through God who strengthens me. Philippians 4:13.

Prayer: Father, you are fully aware of how easy it is for me to fall into the same sins and struggles over and over. You know how often I say I won't do the same thing or fall into the same pit, but I fail to listen to the voice of your Holy Spirit leading me. Please forgive all the times I fail to follow your lead. Help me stay on your path, rather than following my own paths away from you. Thank you I can and do bring these prayers before you in the name of Jesus. Amen.

Think on this: We all have failed in our repentance. The question is what have you done with that failure? Can you relate to the little story in this reading? Why or why not? Have you ever chosen to go a certain direction, even though you knew it was not the best choice? What led to that choice? What can lead you to different choices? Is that what you want? If so, do you know how that can happen?

DAY 82

The Template

"Stan," I said one morning, "one of your encouragements has not worked the way I hoped."

"Which one?" he asked.

"Journaling," I said.

"What about it?"

"You've convinced me of its positive impact on you and your relationship with God," I replied. "I believe it has helped your faith walk. But I've tried to journal with no success. I just can't get in the routine of doing it regularly."

"To get into the routine can definitely be tough," he said.

"You don't have to convince me of that," I said. "I can do it for a couple days, then it's a long time before I get back to it. I'm frustrated. Even when I try, there are some days I just sit there not knowing what to write."

"Maybe I can help," Stan said. "Some time back, I had a similar conversation with a young woman who wanted to journal. Like you, she just couldn't do it consistently. I told her that having a template would probably help."

"What do you mean by a template?"

"Having a set pattern, what to do each time you sit down with your journal. I suggest you start by giving the whole process to God's leading. Even though I've journaled for many years, I start each time by opening my journal and praying over it."

"What do you pray?"

"I ask for God's guidance in opening me to see all He has for me to see in His word. I ask Him to open me to hear what He has to say, and to help me understand. And I ask for His guidance in the words I write, so that I can express what He has shown me."

"Okay," I said, "start with prayer."

"Always a good way to start everything!" Stan said with a smile. "As for your template, I suggest you start small, maybe only a couple of things. You can always add more as you become more comfortable writing. Merely as an example, you could start with the first book in the New Testament, Matthew's gospel. Take it slowly. Read each verse as many times as you need, to get the sense of what it means and what God wants you to apply to your life. Then, begin to write. Be led by the Holy Spirit."

"I like that suggestion. I think I will try Matthew. Any suggestions what to read after that?"

"Sure," Stan replied. "You might consider going to the Old Testament, to the Psalms and Proverbs. Read them the same way: slowly, with your focus on hearing from God. Don't get distracted."

"Distracted by what?" I asked.

"All sorts of things can be a distraction," Stan replied. "I prefer a quiet place with no phone, computer, television, or anything that can get in the way. The day has plenty of time for that stuff. My time with God is my first priority. That's the way I like it, and I think it's the way God likes it."

"Okay," I said. "Start with prayer, read carefully and slowly through each book, little by little, with focus. Then write what I feel God is prompting me to write?"

"Yes."

"How much time are we talking about?"

"I leave that up to God," Stan replied. "He knows better than I do what He has for me to journal about. I start, and He indicates when it's time to finish. Not every day is the same."

"But I thought that's what the template is for: keeping each day the same."

"The same, in the sense of approach," Stan replied. "But each Scripture will have its own application to my life that day, as the Holy Spirit works. However, I can assure you that God's ultimate purpose is always the same."

"What is it?"

"To draw me closer to Himself, in an ever-deepening relationship. If you take this approach," Stan continued, "I can virtually guarantee you'll get into a routine that makes journaling something to eagerly anticipate, rather than something that makes you feel like a failure."

"Thanks," I said. "I'll give it another try."

"Good," Stan replied. "And remember to pray before you start, my friend. Make certain your journaling is being led by God. Pay close attention to His word, as the Holy Spirit uses it. I believe following a template like we've talked about, rather than just impulsively writing about whatever comes to mind, will help keep the focus on God and the relationship He wants to have with you."

Bible verses to consider:
Whatever you do, do all to the glory of God. 1 Corinthians 10:31.

And do not be conformed to this world, but be transformed by the renewing of your mind, that you may prove what the will of God is, that which is good and acceptable and perfect. Romans 12:2.

Prayer: Thank you, Father, for wanting me to have an ever-deepening relationship with you. Thank you that you understand how difficult it is for me to consistently spend time with you or even desire it daily. Please help me when I am distracted by anything that interferes with the relationship you want with me. Thank you, Father, for your constant love and forgiveness. Help me follow your lead into the deeper relationship you want with me. Thank you I can and do bring these prayers before you in the name of Jesus. Amen.

Think on this: Journaling your prayers, devotions, worship, thanksgiving, and study of God's word can have a wonderful impact on relating to God. Have you tried journaling in that way? If so, was it satisfying? Why or why not? If you have not tried journaling, would you like to try? What steps can you take to get started? Following the sort of template that this reading describes may lead you into a deeper relationship with God. Would you like that? Why or why not?

DAY 83

You Never Know Who May Be There

"Stan," I said, "when you think about sharing your faith, do you pre-plan who you'll talk to?"

"You mean do I target a specific person?"

"Yeah, that's it."

"Sometimes I do," Stan responded, "but usually I just follow the example of the apostle Paul."

"What example is that?"

"On one of his missionary journeys, he was in Athens, Greece. He was waiting for Silas and Timothy to join him."

"Athens was probably a pretty nice place to hang out," I said.

"Well, maybe," Stan said, "but it doesn't seem like Paul was just hanging out."

"What was he doing?"

"He was doing a couple different things. One of them is the example I'm talking about. It has a valuable lesson for me, regarding whom I talk to about Jesus, Christianity, my personal faith walk, those sorts of things."

"Is there something Paul was doing that wasn't an example for you?"

"It says in the Book of Acts that Paul was reasoning in the synagogue with the Jews and the God-fearing Gentiles. Going specifically to a synagogue doesn't seem to be what God has for me to do."

"So what is Paul's example for you?"

"He also spent time in the market place every day, reasoning with those who happened to be there. That's the part that indicates the people I should talk to."

"Who's that?"

"Whoever happens to be where I am," Stan replied. "The 'whoever' God puts there, those are the people with whom I'm to share my faith. It's not up to me to determine who God may bring before me. But my part is being prepared to present the gospel to whoever might 'happen' to be there, knowing that God probably engineered the 'happen to be there' part!"

Bible verses to consider:
So he (Paul) was reasoning in the synagogue with the Jews and the God-fearing Gentiles, and in the market place every day with those who happened to be there. Acts of the Apostles 17:17.

Sanctify Christ as Lord in your hearts, always being ready to make a defense to every one who asks you to give an account for the hope that is in you, yet with gentleness and reverence. 1 Peter 3:15.

Let your speech always be with grace, seasoned, as it were, with salt, so that you may know how you should respond to each person. Colossians 4:6.

Prayer: Thank you, Father, for the people you bring before me to hear the truth of the gospel. I confess that way too often I am not prepared to witness to those people, because I have not prepared and am reluctant. Please forgive me. And please help me follow your lead so I am prepared to present the gospel to each person who just "happens" to be there. I know that he or she is there because you have brought them. Please help me to help them know the truth as you intend. Thank you I can and do bring these prayers before you in the name of Jesus. Amen.

Think on this: Are you prepared to present the truth of the gospel at all times and in all places? Why or why not? Do you believe that God brings people into our lives so that we can help them come to belief, and that they don't just "happen" to be there? Why or why not? What will it take for you to be prepared to share with others whenever and wherever the opportunity arises? Do you want to be prepared to do that? Do you know how you can be so prepared?

The Sum of Choices

"Have you ordered yet?" I asked Stan as I sat down.

"Not yet; I was waiting for you. Ricky said there are some specials to consider before we make our choices."

"Seems like there are constant choices to make," I replied. "Sometimes too many choices."

"True," said Stan, "but I think having choices is a good thing."

"In what way?" I asked.

"Gives me an opportunity to really think about what's important. For example, earlier this morning, I was thinking about the contrasts between different people in the Bible, and how they chose to respond to what Jesus said to them."

"Such as what?" I asked.

"When Jesus approached some of the early disciples, He said, 'Follow Me,' and right away they left what they were doing and went with Him."

"Quick obedience," I said.

"Exactly," Stan replied. "On the other hand, there was the fellow called the 'rich young ruler.' You familiar with him?"

"A little," I said. "He's the young man who approached Jesus and asked a question about obtaining eternal life."

"That's right," Stan replied. "And when the young man didn't like Jesus' answer, he went away. And as far as we know, he never did follow Jesus. Some of the disciples went on to be significant players in history, and they continue to have big roles in our lives today. But we never hear from the rich young guy again."

"Very different outcomes," I said.

"Exactly," Stan replied, "and I think the difference is because of the choices they made. Applying this to the person I know best, I think it's fair to say that my life with God is the sum of the choices I've made and continue to make daily."

"Sounds about right," I replied, "except maybe the choices are hourly."

"Or minute-by-minute," Stan said with a smile. "The point is this: it's absolutely essential for me to choose carefully when God shows me what He wants me to be and to do. Once I made the choice to accept His free and gracious gift of salvation, He opened the door to lots of choices I'm to make on this side of eternity before I get on the train."

"Are all those choices up to you?" I asked.

"They are up to me," Stan replied, "but I'm to seek and follow the guidance of the Holy Spirit in making them."

"Sounds good to me," I said. "How about we choose what we're going to have for breakfast?"

Bible verses to consider:
And He said to them, "Follow Me, and I will make you fishers of men." Matthew 4:19.

The young man said to Him, "All these things I have kept; what am I still lacking?" Jesus said to him, "If you wish to be complete, go and sell your possessions and give to the poor, and you shall have treasure in heaven; and come, follow Me." But when the young man heard this statement, he went away grieved; for he was one who owned much property. Matthew 19:21-23.

Work out your salvation with fear and trembling; for it is God who is at work in you, both to will and to work for His good pleasure. Philippians 2:12-13.

Prayer: Thank you, Father, for the gift of being able to spend eternity in your presence when it's time. Thank you, too, for making it clear what you have for me to be and do in this life. I confess that I have not always chosen to follow you, but have often even chosen the opposite direction. Please forgive me for all those wrong choices. And please, Father, help me follow every step of your lead in making the choices you have for me to make, without exception or limit. Thank you I can and do bring these prayers before you in the name of Jesus. Amen.

Think on this: Do you agree that everything in our lives is the result of choices we make? Why or why not? Have you chosen to spend eternity in God's presence when it's time? If no, why? Do you know how to make that choice? If you have the assurance of salvation, what are some choices you face in your faith walk? How might those choices impact the lives and eternal destinations of others?

DAY 85

Couldn't or Wouldn't?

"Yesterday," Stan began, "we talked about choices determining everything for both sides of eternity."

"We did," I said, "contrasting the choices made by some early disciples with the fellow known as the rich young ruler."

"That's right," Stan replied. "And earlier this morning I was drawn back to that story."

"What were you looking at?" I asked.

"Well," Stan said, "you remember how the young man asked Jesus what he needed to do to inherit eternal life. When Jesus gave him a list of things, the young man said, in essence, 'Been there, done that.' Jesus then told him there was one more thing to do. He needed to sell all he had, distribute it to the poor, and follow Jesus."

"The guy was obviously quite rich," I replied. "Getting rid of everything could have been hard."

"That's right," Stan responded. "When the young man heard what Jesus said to him, he became sad, left, and was never heard from again."

"So he likely missed having a personal relationship with God on this side of eternity," I said, "and life eternally with God when it was time. All because he couldn't do what Jesus said."

"I don't think it was so much that he couldn't." Stan replied. "I think it was more he wouldn't."

"You mean he could have done what Jesus said, but chose not to?"

"Exactly," Stan said. "And it's the same thing with me all the time. Not from the standpoint of missing life eternally with God; I've already made that decision. But in terms of life right now. God makes it clear what He has for me to be and do. And way too often my response is basically, 'Thanks, but no thanks.' That young man is described as 'extremely rich,' but he wasn't so rich that he couldn't have done what Jesus said."

"And if he didn't know how to do it," I suggested, "all he had to do was ask Jesus for help."

"Yes, but I think he was more interested in keeping what he had, rather than getting what Jesus offered. I had the same story," Stan added. "Not that I was very rich in worldly goods, but I was very rich in self-focus and did not want to give that up."

"What changed?"

"God finally brought me to the point of seeing that I had to change my focus if I was serious about knowing Him. And if I would let Him, He would do all the heavy lifting to get me to where He wanted me to be, doing what He wanted me to do. If I changed the wouldn't to would, He seemed to say He'd change the couldn't to could!"

Bible verses to consider:
And when Jesus heard this, He said to him, "One thing you still lack; sell all that you possess, and distribute it to the poor, and you shall have treasure in heaven; and come, follow me." But when he had heard these things, he became very sad; for he was extremely rich. Matthew 19:21-22.

For nothing will be impossible with God. Luke 1:37.

With men this is impossible, but with God all things are possible. Matthew 19:26.

Prayer: Thank you, Father, for all you have for me. Please forgive the many times I have not done what you have asked, because there was too much I simply did not want to give up. Thank you that you do not ask the impossible, but whatever you ask, you will enable me to do. Please change all my self-focus to focus on your will and your way. Please help me follow your lead in being and doing what you intend. Thank you I can and do bring these prayers before you in the name of Jesus. Amen.

Think on this: Rather than doing what Jesus said, the rich young ruler went away, never to be heard from again. Can you relate to that story? In what way? Has God asked something of you, and your response has been to turn away? If so, what would it take to change "I won't" into "I will"? In this account, Jesus told His disciples, "With God all things are possible." What might that mean in your life today?

DAY 86

A Relationship with God: Personal but Not Private

"I think I've told you before," Stan said, "that when I first became a Christian, I was mentored by a man who got me moving down the path towards greater spiritual maturity."

"You have told me," I responded, "and you said he was a big help."

"He certainly was," Stan said. "And he once asked me a very pointed question that opened me to see something I had not recognized."

"What was that?"

"He asked if I understood that the essence of Christianity is a personal relationship with God, and not a religion of do's and don'ts for gaining God's favor. He wanted to know if I found comfort in that."

"How did you respond?" I asked.

"I told him I did understand, and that having a personal relationship is at the heart of my faith walk. It's a tremendous comfort to know I don't have to earn God's love."

"And he liked your answer?" I asked.

"Yes," Stan replied, "but he went on to tell me something else."

"What was that?"

"The difference between having a personal relationship with God and having a private relationship with Him."

"Personal versus private," I repeated. "I'm not sure I know what you mean. Aren't they the same thing?"

"Not at all," Stan replied. "For example, have you ever talked with someone about your faith, but found them real reluctant to talk about theirs?"

"More than once," I replied. "I've had people tell me it was a private matter between them and God."

"Me too," Stan said. "And in my humble opinion, that's not the way it's supposed to be."

"Why not?" I asked.

"As with most things," Stan replied, "I like to take my cue from the Bible. In this instance, it seems to me that the apostle Paul addressed this when he told the Corinthians that he was passing on the truth he had received."

"Did he mean the truth of Jesus Christ?" I asked.

"Yes. Paul was not holding back that truth, in a way that precluded others. His faith wasn't private, just between Paul and God. On the contrary," Stan continued, "his first order of business was to share the truth so that others would know Jesus. Can you just imagine where the church would be, if all believers kept their beliefs to themselves because they considered it a private matter between them and God?"

"I suppose the church would have disappeared a long time ago," I said.

"That's more than just a supposition, my friend," Stan replied. "I think it's a fact. As personal as it is, God wants my relationship with Him to be public. Then others will know such a possibility exists for them, too."

"Seems to me that sharing the truth is the only way the church is going to grow."

"That's it," Stan said, "and not only growth in numbers, but individuals will grow in their personal relationship with God."

Bible verses to consider:
For I delivered to you as of first importance what I also received, that Christ died for our sins according to the Scriptures, and that He was buried, and that He was raised on the third day according to the Scriptures. 1 Corinthians 15:3-4.

How then shall they call upon Him in whom they have not believed? And how shall they believe in Him whom they have not heard? And how shall they hear without a preacher? And how will they preach unless they are sent? Romans 10:14-15.

Prayer: Thank you, Father, for providing the way for me to have a personal relationship with you, through the life, death, and resurrection of Jesus Christ. Thank you for this free and gracious gift. I confess that too often I fail to share this gift with others, hiding behind the notion that it is private between you and me. Please help me to openly share and demonstrate our relationship, so others may also know you deeply. Thank you I can and do bring these prayers before you in the name of Jesus. Amen.

Think on this: Have you accepted what Christ Jesus did through His life, death, and resurrection? If so, are you also pursuing a growing, personal relationship with God? If no, why not? If you are, is it as open and public as you think God wants? What would happen to the church if believers kept their faith a private matter? Would it be as vibrant as it should be? Do you need help in being more open about your faith? If so, do you know how to find that help?

DAY 87

Giving and Getting Samples

"I went to the Big Box Wholesale Club yesterday," Stan began, "and I experienced a real truth to strengthen my walk with God."

"At Big Box?" I asked. "What was that all about?"

"I was in one of the food aisles," Stan replied, "and I saw something I hadn't seen before: dried mangoes. I picked up a package and read about the nutritional aspects and all that stuff. The package even had a window to see what was inside. If you've never seen dried mangos, I can tell you they aren't real pretty."

"Never seen them," I said with a smile.

"Just then," Stan continued, "another shopper stopped and told me there was a person at the end of the aisle giving out samples. She said they were real tasty, and she was picking up a package to buy."

"So, did you get a sample?"

"I did," Stan replied. "Tasted real good, so I bought a package. Love those dried mangoes! They're a good snack."

"Giving out samples is a great marketing approach," I said.

"Sure is," Stan responded. "And that's the part of the story that strengthens and encourages my walk with God."

"How so?" I asked.

"Rather than just wondering about something, if I can get a 'sample' of what God is doing in another person's life, my walk with God is strengthened."

"What do you mean by 'get a sample'?"

"I mean seeing the manifestation of Christ in that person," Stan explained. "Also, if I share samples of what God is doing in and through me, it may help another person's walk with Him."

"You mean they might want more for themselves?" I asked, "such as knowing more about Him? And growing more?"

"Exactly, my friend," Stan said. "Giving out and getting samples of what God is doing. I think that's why it's so vital for me to be around fellow Christians. I can listen and learn what they have to say about what God is doing in their lives. It's essential for me," Stan concluded, "to be part of the church and involved in at least one fellowship group. Not just attend, but really hear from others. Also be prepared to share what is going on in my own walk with God. I need to give out free samples of His goodness, as I continue on the path from conversion to transformation."

Bible verses to consider:
What we have seen and heard we proclaim to you also, that you also may have fellowship with us; and indeed our fellowship is with the Father, and with His son Jesus Christ. 1 John 1:3.

Let your light shine before men in such a way that they may see your good works and glorify your Father who is in heaven. Matthew 5:16.

Prayer: Thank you, Father, for allowing me to experience what you are doing in and through fellow believers. Thank you for the encouragement that you provide in that way. Far too often I am reluctant to share with others what you are doing because I think they may not be interested. Please forgive that foolishness, and please help me know that they, too, want to be encouraged by hearing what you are doing. Please, Father, help me follow your lead so that all such sharing is done and received in accordance with your will. Thank you I can and do bring these prayers before you in the name of Jesus. Amen.

Think on this: Do you enjoy hearing from others what God is doing in their lives? Why or why not? Do you like to share what God is doing in and through you? Why or why not? Have you ever experienced listening to another person tell what God is doing and wondered why God is not doing the same thing in your life? If so, what did you do? What should be the purpose of such sharing? How does it glorify God?

DAY 88

Looking for the Wanderer

"I was in Matthew's gospel again this morning," Stan began. "As I was journaling, some of what Jesus said brought back a vivid memory of my early days as a Christian."

"What was it?" I asked.

"He was talking to His disciples and using the analogy of a shepherd who had one hundred sheep, but one of them wandered away."

"I remember that story," I said. "The shepherd left the ninety-nine to go look for the one."

"You're right, my friend," Stan replied. "And I thought of my early days, being involved with a small church. I was having trouble getting plugged in. I just didn't feel I was part of the church. So I stopped attending after a few weeks. Not too long after that, the pastor came to my house to ask if everything was okay."

"He came to your house?" I responded. "Did that embarrass you?"

"It didn't embarrass me in the least," Stan replied. "I knew the pastor reached out to me from genuine concern. He and I had a long discussion. I shared honestly what I was feeling about the church, and he gave me some excellent counsel. By the time he left, I felt very encouraged."

"Did you go back to that church?" I asked.

"I did," Stan replied. "Not only did I return, but as I got more involved, I really began to grow in my relationship with God. I can only guess where I'd now be in my relationship with God, if that pastor hadn't reached out in love to see where I might have wandered."

"A good reminder," I replied, "to be on the alert for others in the church who may need encouragement in their walk, so they don't go wandering off in a direction God does not intend for them."

"You're right, my friend," Stan responded. "Keep an eye out for those who may have wandered."

Bible verses to consider:
What do you think? If any man has a hundred sheep, and one of them has gone astray, does he not leave the ninety-nine on the mountains and go and search for the one that is straying? Matthew 18:12.

I have gone astray like a lost sheep; seek Thy servant, for I do not forget Thy commandments. Psalm 119:176.

For you were continually straying like sheep, but now you have returned to the Shepherd and Guardian of your souls. 1 Peter 2:25.

Prayer: Thank you, Father, for sending your people to look for those who may have wandered away from you. I want to be part of what you want, reaching out to those who need encouragement in their faith walk. I confess that too often I am not the encourager you intend. Please forgive me for that. And please, Father, lead me in accordance with your will in reaching out, so anyone who may have gone astray is encouraged to come back into your fold. Please lead and help me follow. Thank you I can and do bring these prayers before you in the name of Jesus. Amen.

Think on this: Can you relate to this story of how Stan wandered away because he did not feel a part of the church body? Have you ever been in that situation? If yes, what happened? Did someone come looking for you? Do you know people who have wandered away and may need encouragement to return? If yes, what would it look like for you to reach out to them? Do you want to do that? If no, why? If yes, how are you going to do that?

DAY 89

The Open House

"One of our neighbors has done some extensive remodeling to their house. They had an open house Saturday so we could all see."

"Nice?" I responded.

"Amazing," Stan replied. "Their house is really transformed, totally different from the original."

"Did they do the work themselves?" I asked.

"No," Stan replied. "They hired that firm over on Abbott Drive to do the design and all the reconstruction. I'd say that firm is really good at what they do. And you know something else? Seeing that neighbor's remodel made several others talk about having their own houses redesigned." Stan paused, then added, "Just like Jesus."

"Just like Jesus?" I asked. "What does an open house have to do with Him?"

"Everything!" Stan said. "Jesus is clearly in the remodeling business."

"What do you mean?"

"I'll use the example I know best," said Stan. "My own life. There came a time when it was brought to my attention that I needed a remodel. The Bible calls it 'transformation.'"

"Who brought that to your attention?" I asked.

"God. Through His word, through the voice of the Holy Spirit, and through other people and circumstances, God made it clear I was not who He intended me to be. As well, I was not doing what God intended while He left me on this side of eternity."

"So," I said, "how did you begin the remodeling project on your life?"

"Confession," Stan replied. "I had to come before God totally open and surrendered, with the admission that some serious re-design and construction were needed."

"Then what?" I asked.

"Repentance," Stan said. "I had to do something with my confession. Otherwise, it would be like neighbors deciding to remodel their house, but not getting the work done. A home remodel doesn't happen all by itself. Same with me."

"And I guess it would be the same with me," I said. "I have to do something after admitting something needs to be done."

"That's more than a guess," Stan said. "I'd put it in the category of being absolutely essential!"

"Okay," I replied. "Say I acknowledge I need a remodeled life. And further, I go ahead with that remodel. What then?"

"God is apt to have an open house," Stan said, "so everyone can come and see what He has done. That way others may decide they want some remodeling in their own lives."

Bible verses to consider:
Come and see the works of God, who is awesome in His deeds towards the sons of men. Psalm 66:5.

And do not be conformed to this world, but be transformed by the renewing of your mind, that you may prove what the will of God is, that which is good and acceptable and perfect. Romans 12:2.

But we all, with unveiled face beholding as in a mirror the glory of the Lord, are being transformed into the same image from glory to glory, just as from the Lord, The Spirit. 2 Corinthians 3:18.

Repent therefore and return, that your sins may be wiped away, in order that times of refreshing may come with the presence of the Lord. Acts of the Apostles 3:19.

Prayer: Thank you, Father, for your provision of confession and repentance. Thank you for loving me enough to show me when I need remodeling and transformation in my life and in my relationship with you. I confess that too often I do not listen to you when you tell me I need to change. Please help me to confess and repent so that you can complete the transformational remodeling you want. Thank you I can and do bring these prayers before you in the name of Jesus. Amen.

Think on this: Does your life and relationship with God need some remodeling? If so, what are you going to do about it? Is it sufficient to admit that some work is needed? If no, what needs to follow and how does that get done? Is that something you want? Can you do it on your own or do you need some help? If you need help, where will it come from?

DAY 90

It Takes More Than Talk

"Near our family farm," Stan began, "there was a small town."

"How small?" I asked.

"You'd laugh if I told you," Stan replied.

"Was there much there?" I asked.

"The basics. The schools were there. The post office, a grocery store, a hardware store, a co-operative where the farmers sold their crops, things like that. And there was one place that was really the gathering place for the farmers. It was called Henry's Corner, really a multipurpose place. Gas station, mechanic shop, and general store."

"I like general stores," I said. "You can find most anything in them."

"And at Henry's," Stan said, "you could buy a candy bar, ice cream cone, a soft drink, or an adult beverage if you were old enough and so inclined. You could buy a magazine, or even get your hair cut."

"Sounds like it had just about everything a small community needed," I said.

"Sure did," said Stan. "I thought about Henry's when my wife and I had Chinese food last night."

"Henry sold Chinese food, too?" I asked.

Stan laughed. "No, but there was a Chinese proverb on the back of the menu that reminded me of someone who always hung out at Henry's."

"What was the proverb?" I asked.

"Talk does not cook rice."

"And how did that remind you of someone at Henry's?" I responded.

"There was a farmer who always seemed to be there, every time we stopped. As well, he always seemed to say the same thing."

"What was that?"

"How much work he had to do," Stan said.

"Talking about it rather than doing it?"

"Exactly," Stan said. "And it was the same thing with my faith walk for way too long. And it can still be a problem if I don't watch out."

"How so?" I asked.

"I would talk about what I needed to do in order to have a deeper relationship with God," Stan replied, "but it was talk rather than doing anything about it."

"Talk rather than walk?" I said.

"Yes. And that proverb says it well: the rice won't get cooked by just talking about cooking it. I need to focus on being and doing, not just talking about it!"

Bible verses to consider:
In all labor there is profit, but mere talk leads only to poverty. Proverbs 14:23.

Draw near to God and He will draw near to you. James 4:8.

Prayer: Thank you, Father, for wanting to have an ever-deepening relationship with me. Thank you, too, for showing me that such a relationship will not happen by merely talking about it. I need to pursue a deeper relationship with you, knowing that as I choose to draw near to you, your response will be to draw near to me. I confess that too often I do not go beyond talking about having a closer relationship with you. Please, Father, help me follow every step of your lead into as deep and close a relationship with you as is possible. Help me go beyond talking, to doing and being. Thank you I can and do bring these prayers before you in the name of Jesus. Amen.

Think on this: How do you get beyond just talking about a closer relationship with God? Is this something you want? Why or why not? If so, do you know how to pursue that? Do you agree that if you draw closer to God, He will draw closer to you? Have you ever experienced that? If no, would you like to? Do you know how that can happen?

DAY 91

Just Don't Do It

"You look kind of somber this morning," I said to Stan as I sat down. "What's going on?"

"I was reading in James' letter this morning," he said, "the part where he wrote about being carried away by lust into sin, death, and the like. I was thinking how that truth impacts so many people, including me."

"Heavy subject," I replied.

"Heavy, indeed," he said. "But the good news is that there's a pretty simple solution."

"Simple? How so?"

"Do you know the best way for something not to happen?" Stan asked. Then, without giving me time to reply, he said, "Just don't do it!"

"Don't do it?"

"Yes," Stan responded. "Abstinence works every time. That applies to everything, whatever it is. If I don't want to get a speeding ticket, abstain from speeding. And," he added with a smile, "if we don't want to miss breakfast, abstain from talking until we've place our order!"

We both told Ricky we'd like blueberry pancakes and coffee. After he had gone, Stan continued. "James wrote about being carried away and enticed by lust. Once that happens, the lust gives birth to sin. And then, when the sin is accomplished, death is the result. It may not be eternal death, but it can certainly be the death of my spiritual growth on this side of eternity. Slow learner that I am, it took me way too long to accept the truth of what James wrote. If I choose not to be enticed by the world, the flesh, and the devil, there's no chance of lust turning into sin."

"Yeah," I responded, "I can see that. But it's easier said than done."

"I don't disagree," Stan replied. "It's not easy. But don't forget that with every temptation, God provides the way out. I just have to choose to embrace His provision."

"So the answer is making the right choice?" I asked. "Is that what you're saying?"

"That's it," Stan replied. "And I have to be told the same thing every day, often many times."

"What same thing?" I asked.

"Just don't do it!" Stan exclaimed. "Don't start down that road. Abstain from lust. Don't give it a chance to grow. Take the thoughts of lust captive to the obedience of Christ. Abstinence works every time. Give it a try. That's what the Holy Spirit says to me all the time. I just need to listen, obey, and choose to abstain. And remember, my friend, it is a choice."

Bible verses to consider:
But each one is tempted when he is carried away and enticed by his own lust. Then when lust has been conceived, it gives birth to sin; and when sin is accomplished, it brings forth death. James 1:14-15.

No temptation has overtaken you but such as is common to man; and God is faithful, who will not allow you to be tempted beyond what you are able, but with the temptation will provide the way of escape also, that you may be able to endure it. 1 Corinthians 10:13.

For the wages of sin is death, but the free gift of God is eternal life in Christ Jesus our Lord. Romans 6:23.

Prayer: Thank you, Father, that you have the remedy for all my lusts that can lead to sin and the death of my spiritual growth. I confess that too often I do not heed your word and your voice, telling me to do what works every time: simply abstain from allowing lust to do what it wants to do in my life. Please forgive me. And please help me follow your lead away from the trap that is laid for me by the world, the flesh, and the devil. Help me choose to abstain and claim your every provision away from temptation. Thank you I can and do bring these prayers before you in the name of Jesus. Amen.

Think on this: Whether or not we will spend eternity in God's presence is a choice. Have you made the choice to be with Him? If no, why? Do you know how to make that choice? Being enticed by lust that leads to sin is also a choice. Do you agree with that? Why or why not? If you find yourself being enticed by the same lust over and over, do you know that God has the help you need? Do you know how to ask for His help?

DAY 92

The Career Counselor

"We have some new neighbors," Stan began. "We had them over for dinner last night to get acquainted."

"Nice people?" I asked.

"Very," Stan replied. "I think we're going to be great friends. The wife is a career counselor over at the college."

"So she works with students?" I asked. "Helps them figure out what kind of career they want, what classes to take, that sort of thing?"

"That's it," Stan said. "She said she starts with giving them a form to fill out, with blanks for what they might want to pursue."

"Start by filling in the blanks," I said. "That makes sense."

"It does. We got talking about our own career paths, and she asked how I figured out what I wanted to be."

"You had an answer for her?"

"I did," Stan replied. "I told her after growing up on a farm, I knew I didn't want to be a farmer. My dad loved the work, and my older brother too, but it wasn't for me. I needed to find something else. I had several starts, stops, and changed directions before I hit upon what I wanted to be. All that was in my pre-Christian days. I didn't know about Jesus' career counseling back then."

"Jesus' career counseling? What's that?"

"Well, it's not exactly called that, but Matthew mentions something that points in that direction."

"How so?"

"It's where Jesus was calling His first disciples," Stan replied. "He was walking by the Sea of Galilee and saw two brothers, Peter and Andrew. They were fishermen."

"I remember that story," I said. "Jesus told them to follow Him, and they dropped everything and did so."

"That's right," Stan replied, "but there's something else in that story that I think is important about knowing what to do."

"What's that?" I asked.

"Jesus said, 'Follow Me, and I will make you fishers of men.' Notice that He didn't say, 'Follow Me and be fishers of men.' In other words, Jesus would mold, shape, and transform them into a new career. It wasn't something they would do on their own. And," Stan continued, "it was the same for me once I became a Christian. There came a point where I had to give up all that I had planned to pursue apart from God. I had to choose to follow and allow Him to make me into whatever He wanted. He would fill in the blanks."

"Fill in the blanks?" I said. "How so?"

"With me, you, and everyone who calls on His name, He will make us into whatever He wants. It's as if He says, 'Follow Me and I will make you_____,' then He fills in the blank. The important part is following and doing what He wants. He is the Counselor, for careers and everything else!"

Bible verses to consider:
And He said to them, "Follow Me, and I will make you fishers of men." Matthew 4:19.

For a child will be born to us, a son will be given to us; and the government will rest on His shoulders; and His name will be called Wonderful Counselor, Mighty God, Eternal Father, Prince of Peace. Isaiah 9:6.

But the Helper, the Holy Spirit, whom the Father will send in My name, He will teach you all things, and bring to your remembrance all I have said to you. John 14:26.

Or do you not know that your body is a temple of the Holy Spirit who is in you, whom you have from God, and that you are not you own? For you have been bought with a price; therefore glorify God in your body. 1 Corinthians 6:19-20.

Prayer: Thank you, Father, that you want to lead me to where you want me to be in my relationship with you. Thank you for sending the Holy Spirit, the Helper and Counselor, for me to follow. I confess that I often choose to go my own way and don't take you and your will into account in making decisions about "my" life. Please forgive that foolishness, and help me follow your wise, loving, and magnificent counsel. Thank you I can and do bring these prayers before you in the name of Jesus. Amen.

Think on this: Do you rely on God's leading for decisions in your life? Why or why not? Do you see a difference between "big" and "small" decisions in deciding what to bring to God? If so, do you think that distinction is valid? Does God? What would it look like for you to follow God in whatever He wants to do in and through you? Is that something you would like? Why or why not? If you would like that for your life, do you know how it can happen?

DAY 93

Dreading or Smiling at the Future?

"Good morning, Stan," I said, sitting down. "What's up?"

"Before you got here," Stan replied, "I was talking with Ricky about how we are living in some pretty scary times. Lots of uncertainty with all that's going on."

"You've got that right," I said. "Some days I don't even want to look at the news, for fear that something worse has happened."

"Yeah," Stan replied, "it's easy to get dragged down. But earlier this morning I saw a single verse in the Book of Proverbs that gives a really encouraging outlook."

"Good," I replied. "I can use an encouraging outlook. What did you see?"

"The last chapter of Proverbs is mainly about the qualities of an excellent wife. But I think verse 25 applies to everyone, including me."

"What's it say?"

"That she smiles at the future," Stan replied.

"Smiles at the future," I repeated. "That is a good outlook. How can I do that?"

"I think there are two main ways," Stan said. "First, there's the long-term future. Eternity is about as long term as you can get, and the idea of spending eternity with God causes me to smile."

"From the assurance of salvation?" I asked.

"Exactly," Stan replied. "I know where I'm going when I get on the train. How can I not smile?"

"Okay," I said, "that's one. What's the second reason to smile at the future?"

"Jesus said that eternal life is being able to know Him and His Father. I think that occurs here, on this side of eternity. When I think about the Lord God Almighty, and the wonder of being able to pursue knowing Him, His purposes, and all that He has for me, how can I not smile?"

"Focusing on the Father, the Son, and the Holy Spirit," I replied. "gives the reason to smile. Is that what you're saying?"

"You got it, my friend," Stan said. "Satan wants me to focus on him, the world, and the flesh. If I do that, there's not a whole lot to smile about. But as I focus on God and all He has for me, knowing beyond a shadow of doubt that His will is going to be done and His purposes are going to be accomplished, I can, and I do, smile at the future!"

"That," I replied, "is a whole lot better than dreading it!"

Bible verses to consider:
She smiles at the future. Proverbs 31:25.

This is the day which the Lord has made; let us rejoice and be glad in it. Psalm 118:24.

Do not be grieved, for the joy of the Lord is your strength. Nehemiah 8:10.

And this is eternal life, that they may know Thee, the only true God, and Jesus Christ whom Thou hast sent. John 17:3.

Prayer: Thank you, Father, for all you have for me to smile about. I smile when I think of spending eternity in your presence, and I smile because I can pursue knowing you and your Son more deeply on this side of eternity. There is much in this world that can cause me sadness or worry. Please help me focus only on you and your will and purposes, and not on the world, the flesh, and the devil, which only drag me down. Thank you I can and do bring these prayers before you in the name of Jesus. Amen.

Think on this: If we allow our focus to be on the world, there is much that can cause us not to smile. Do you agree with that? Why or why not? Do you find yourself smiling at or dreading the future? Do you have the assurance of salvation that causes you to smile? If no, why? Does your growing relationship with God cause you to smile? Why or why not? Would you like to be able to smile at the future? If so, do you know how that can happen?

DAY 94

Choosing Not to Look

"I was reading in Matthew's gospel last night," I said to Stan one morning.

"Anything interesting?" he asked.

"Yeah," I said, "both interesting and somewhat bothersome."

"What were you looking at?"

"Where Jesus told some people to rip their eye out and throw it away if it caused them to sin," I replied.

"You're right," Stan replied, "tough talk. But it wasn't uncommon for Jesus to say things in a strong way to make a simple point."

"What's simple about telling someone to rip their eye out and throw it away?"

"Well," said Stan, "I think the basic point Jesus was making had to do with stumbling into sin and how destructive sin can be in a person's life. I can say from too much personal experience that sin can, indeed, have a destructive impact on a life. I think Jesus was warning that if something I look at causes me to stumble into sin, I better watch out and pay closer attention. He knows there are serious consequences of looking at the wrong things."

"Okay," I said, "rather than rip my eye out and throw it away, I should beware of what I look at. Is that what you're saying?"

"That's it," Stan replied. "And you know as well as I do that there's a lot of stuff to look at that can cause stumbling into sin. Books, magazines, movies, television, the internet. You could even include certain people that I shouldn't be looking at in certain ways. This list goes on and on."

"So if I'm not constantly aware of how I look at something or someone, I guess there's the danger I could be headed for trouble."

"I'd say it's pretty certain," said Stan. "This sort of stumbling into sin isn't about losing my salvation, but about missing who God intends for me to be this side of eternity. And if I miss that, it may cause another person to stumble. I don't want that! So I call upon the Holy Spirit to help me in whatever way necessary."

Bible verses to consider:
And if your right eye makes you stumble, tear it out, and throw it from you; for it is better for you that one of the parts of your body perish, than for your body to be thrown into hell. Matthew 5:29.

No temptation has overtaken you but such as is common to man; and God is faithful, who will not allow you to be tempted beyond what you are able, but with the temptation will provide the way of escape also, that you may endure it. 1 Corinthians 10:13.

It would be better for him if a millstone were hung around his neck and he were thrown into the sea, than that he should cause one of these little ones to stumble. Luke 17:2.

Prayer: Thank you, Father, for the warnings set forth in your word that lead me to avoid the consequences of sin. You know how often I am tempted to look at things and people in ways you do not want, that may cause me to stumble into sin. I need and I ask for your help to avoid stumbling in ways that will impact who I am and what I do for you. Thank you I can and do bring these prayers before you in the name of Jesus. Amen.

Think on this: Do you agree that the world, the flesh, and the devil have all sorts of things for us to look at that can cause us to stumble into sin? Why or why not? Are there particular things you look at, in ways that have caused you to stumble? If so, what happened? Do you want to avoid stumbling in the future? Why or why not? If you do, are you familiar with the help that is available? Do you want that help?

DAY 95

Professing yet Denying

“Stan,” I asked, “do you think it’s possible for a person to profess they know God but deny Him at the same time?”

“Sure do,” Stan replied. “And I have ample evidence to back that up!”

“What kind of evidence?” I asked.

“Me,” he said.

“What do you mean?”

“There’s no doubt in my mind,” Stan said, “that I will get on the train when the time is right, to spend the rest of eternity in God’s presence. And there’s no doubt in my mind that God has left me on this side of eternity to be and to do what He intends while I wait for the train.”

“Okay,” I said, “I understand that. But what about the denying God part?”

“That’s when what I am and what I do are opposite from what I profess,” he said. “And the apostle Paul addresses this very thing in his letter to Titus. Paul had left Titus on the island of Crete, to work with the church there.”

“What did Paul write?” I asked.

“He wrote about people who said one thing about their belief in God but acted in ways that showed the exact opposite. And that’s where I fit in, way too often.”

“Kind of like not fitting the old saying, Walk the walk, don’t just talk the talk?”

“Not just kind of,” he said, “but exactly, my friend! What I say about being God’s, what I say about being transformed, and what I say about growing in my knowledge of God has to match what I am and what I do.”

"What if it doesn't?" I asked.

"If my walk and talk are not in agreement," he concluded, "it's time for me to open up and allow the Holy Spirit to do some serious talking to me! Serious talking, followed by my serious listening, serious repenting, and serious obedience!"

Bible verses to consider:
They profess to know God, but by their deeds they deny Him. Titus 1:16.

And a certain servant-girl, seeing him (Peter) as he sat by the firelight, and looking intently at him, said, "This man was with Him (Jesus) too." But he denied it, saying, "Woman, I do not know Him." Luke 22:56-57.

For all have sinned and fall short of the glory of God, being justified as a gift by His grace through the redemption which is in Christ Jesus. Romans 3:23-24.

For by grace you have been saved through faith; and that not of yourselves, it is a gift of God; not as a result of works, that no one should boast. Ephesians 2:8-9.

Prayer: Thank you, Father, for the truth of your word that reminds me where you want me to be, and where I fall short, in my relationship with you. Thank you for the finished work of Christ Jesus on the cross that gives me the assurance of spending eternity with you when it's time. Thank you, too, for the presence of the Holy Spirit in me to show me how you want me to live on this side of eternity. I confess that too often my walk with you does not match what I profess about our relationship and my commitment to you. Please forgive me and help me make my walk with you match my talk about you. Thank you I can and do bring these prayers before you in the name of Jesus. Amen.

Think on this: Is there a disconnect between what you profess about your relationship with God and what you do with that relationship? Why or why not? If your walk does not match your talk, is that something you want to change? If so, do you know how to pursue change?

DAY 96

The Desert of Unbelief

"I was reading in the letter to the Hebrews this morning," Stan said, "where the writer was focusing on the Jews wandering in the desert for forty years."

"Forty years wandering around a desert," I replied. "I'm not sure I've ever understood what that was about."

"I think the writer nailed it by saying they weren't able to enter the Promised Land because of unbelief."

"As simple as that?" I asked. "Their unbelief?"

"As simple and as complicated as that!" Stan replied. "And I can certainly relate."

"In what way?"

"I wandered around my own desert of unbelief for way too long. But eventually I accepted the truth of what God has done for me, through the finished work of Jesus on the cross. That finished work has given me the assurance of spending the rest of eternity with God when it's time. And God has given me the presence of the Holy Spirit on this side of eternity, to guide, help, and counsel me in entering God's ongoing work."

"I guess there's no need to keep wandering," I replied, "if the ability to stop is readily available."

"Bingo and amen!" Stan exclaimed. "That's not just a guess; it's the truth! And often, a person stops wandering in unbelief only when someone who has found the way out of that desert tells them how. The Jews wandered for forty years, because they failed to believe and obey all that God told them."

"Just think," I said, "of all the people out there wandering in their own desert of unbelief. Why don't they know how to stop wandering?"

"Because no one has bothered to tell them," Stan replied. "Are there people you need to tell, so they might believe and stop wandering?"

Bible verses to consider:
And so we see that they were not able to enter because of unbelief. Hebrews 3:19.

How then shall they call upon Him in whom they have not believed? And how shall they believe in Him whom they have not heard? And how shall they hear without a preacher? Romans 10:14.

And even if our gospel is veiled, it is veiled to those who are perishing, in whose case the god of this world has blinded the minds of the unbelieving, that they might not see the light of the gospel of the glory of Christ, who is the image of God. 2 Corinthians 4:3-4.

Prayer: Thank you, Father, for the truth of your provision of life eternally with you through the finished work of Jesus. Thank you for those who told me the truth, so I could accept it by faith and stop wandering in the desert of unbelief. You bring people before me each day who are wandering the way I was. Too often I fail to tell them the truth so they, too, can stop wandering. Please forgive me. And please help me follow your lead in telling everyone you want me to tell, so they can stop wandering in their desert of unbelief. Thank you I can and do bring these prayers before you in the name of Jesus. Amen.

Think on this: Have you stopped wandering in the desert of unbelief? If no, why? If you have stopped wandering, can you point to a specific person who told you how? If you are no longer wandering, are there people in your life who need to hear how they, too, can stop wandering in their own desert of unbelief? Are you willing to do that? Why or why not? If you are willing, do you know how to do that? If not, do you know how to learn?

DAY 97

How to Know What to Obey

"I just love reading about the early church," Stan said.

"What do you mean by 'early church'?" I asked.

"It's the time right after Jesus went to the cross, died, was buried, was resurrected, and then ascended into heaven," Stan replied. "It's recorded in the book called Acts of the Apostles."

"What is it you like about that time?" I asked.

"The church was getting off on the right foot," Stan replied. "The Holy Spirit was clearly leading. If they didn't get it right, the church might not have survived. I think there's a lot for the present-day church to learn from what the early church experienced."

"Like what?" I asked.

"Many, many things, but the one I was focusing on this morning is a prime example, not only for the church in general, but for me in particular."

"What were you looking at?"

"Peter and the other apostles were boldly talking about Jesus and what He had accomplished through His life, death, and resurrection. The Jewish leaders didn't like what the apostles were saying, so they had them arrested and did all sorts of things to prevent them talking about Jesus."

"Did the apostles stop?" I asked.

"No," Stan said, "and the reason they didn't is important for me."

"What's that?"

"They said they were obligated to obey God, not men."

"Sounds like a reasonable thing to say."

"Yes, and I agree completely. And there's something that goes without saying, but I'll say it anyway: How am I going to obey what God says, rather than what others tell me, if I don't know what God says?"

"And how will you know that?" I asked.

"By reading God's word and listening to the voice of the Holy Spirit," Stan replied. "If I don't do that, there's no way I'm going to know how to do what He says. I'll be sucked into thinking that what other people say is what I'm supposed to obey."

"And," I said, "if those others aren't in touch with what God says, they may be telling you or me the wrong thing. Is that what I'm supposed to watch for?"

"You got it, my friend," Stan replied.

Bible verses to consider:
But Peter and the apostles answered and said, "We must obey God rather than men." Acts of the Apostles 5:29.

But Peter and John answered and said to them, "Whether it is right in the sight of God to give heed to you rather than to God, you be the judge; for we cannot stop speaking what we have seen and heard." Acts of The Apostles 4:19-20.

Prayer: Thank you, Father, that you make it clear what you have for me to obey. Thank you, too, for making it clear that I cannot know what you say and what to obey unless I spend time reading your word and listening to the Holy Spirit's voice. Please help me to know what you have for me to obey, so that I will not get sidetracked listening to the voice of others who don't know you. Help me to obey you at all costs. Thank you I can and do bring these prayers before you in the name of Jesus. Amen.

Think on this: Is it possible to obey God without knowing what you are supposed to obey? Why or why not? It can be difficult living in today's world, where many do not know God and His word, but seek to impose their views that are contrary to God. If you have not been confronted by that, you will. How will you respond? Do you agree that we are to obey God and not men? Why or why not?

DAY 98

Where's Your Antioch?

"From time to time," Stan began, "we've talked about the importance of having a personal testimony to share with other people."

"We have," I responded. "It's easier to share the truth of God's gift of salvation if I can tell another person how I came to faith."

"Exactly," Stan replied. "No one can argue about what you or I have personally experienced. I thought of this while reading in Acts this morning."

"Something about sharing your personal testimony?" I asked.

"Well, not exactly, but there's a statement that I consider essential to my personal testimony."

"What's that?"

"It says that those in the early church were first called Christians in Antioch."

"So?" I asked.

"I think an essential part of my personal testimony," Stan explained, "is to be able to tell others where I first knew I could be called a Christian. Without relating that part of my experience, others might wonder if I considered my conversion all that important."

"Are you saying it might give the impression that your conversion didn't matter, if where it happened wasn't important enough to remember?"

"Yeah," said Stan. "As I've mentioned before, it took me a long time to come to faith. It was a gradual process, until one day there was a moment of belief.

My experience, while not unusual, was different from a lot of people. Some believe the truth the first time they hear it."

"I remember that you once called yourself a slow learner," I said with a smile.

"Slow, indeed," Stan replied. "That moment of belief is what I call 'my Antioch.' And I can assure you, it was the most important thing that ever happened to me. I was able to be called a Christian, and I'll never forget that moment, because it changed forever my eternal destination and my life on this side of eternity! How could I possibly forget the location of my Antioch?"

Bible verse to consider:
The disciples were first called Christians in Antioch. Acts of the Apostles 11:26.

Prayer: Thank you, Father, for your gracious and free gift of salvation through the finished work of Christ Jesus on the cross. Thank you for the moment in time when, by faith, I accepted the truth of your provision. Thank you that it changed forever my eternal destination and my life on this side of eternity. Thank you it is an important part of my personal testimony, and please use it so that others may have their life and eternal destination changed. Thank you I can and do bring these prayers before you in the name of Jesus. Amen.

Think on this: Do you think that a personal testimony is important? Why or why not? If you are a Christian, what details can you recall from your conversion? How would you describe your acceptance of God's free and gracious gift of salvation? In what ways could specific details of your testimony impact someone who has not yet become a Christian? Is that important to you? To God? Why or why not?

DAY 99

The Overflow

"As you know," Stan began, "we've been having an unusual amount of rain."

"By the bucket," I replied. "Never seen so much rain. Maybe it's time to build the ark!"

"Could be," Stan said. "Yesterday I drove to Johnsonville to talk with the pastor of the community church. On the way over the mountain, I went by the dam on Johnson Creek. It was filled to the brim, with water overflowing down the spillway. Several people had stopped and were watching all the water pouring out. They'd probably never seen anything like that."

"Must have been quite a sight," I replied.

"It was. And it made me think how my life is to be just like that."

"In what way?"

"I am to be so filled with the presence of the Holy Spirit that He overflows, and people stop and look."

"Stop and look? How so?"

"I am to receive the Holy Spirit and be filled as fully as possible," Stan said, "so that His fruit is manifested in and through me, affecting the lives of others, who hopefully will see something new to them."

"You mean seeing and maybe wanting it for themselves?"

"Yes," said Stan, "and perhaps asking how they might have the same thing. That could lead to changed lives and changed eternal destinations!"

"But if the Holy Spirit flows out of you, so that others see His abundant work, won't you be emptied?"

"Nope," Stan replied, "it's really an overflow. And an overflow means there is a constant supply coming in. With the dam on Johnson Creek, the overflow will eventually end when the rain stops. But my life is to be continually filled with the 'rain' of the Holy Spirit. And His overflow just keeps overflowing!"

"To make a difference," I replied, "in those people who stop to take a look."

"That's it," Stan said. "Because they see the overflowing of the Holy Spirit, they may want to know why, which may lead them to ask, 'Is that something I can have?' And that may lead them to salvation, and to a different life because of that salvation."

"All because of the overflow!"

Bible verses to consider:
And I will ask the Father, and He will give you another Helper, that He may be with you forever; that is the Spirit of truth, whom the world cannot receive, because it does not behold Him or know Him, but you know Him because He abides with you, and will be with you. John 14:16-17.

Be filled with the Holy Spirit. Ephesians 5:18.

But the fruit of the Spirit is love, joy, peace, patience, kindness, goodness, faithfulness, gentleness, self-control; against such things there is no law. Galatians 5:22-23.

And the disciples were continually filled with joy and with the Holy Spirit. Acts of the Apostles 13:52.

Prayer: Thank you, Father, for your gift of the Holy Spirit, who lives within me to guard, guide, and help me as I wait for the train. Thank you that there is an unlimited supply of His presence in me, so that He can overflow out of my life. I confess that too often I do not allow myself to be filled, so there is less evidence of His presence for others to see. Please help me follow your lead so there is, indeed, an overflow of the Holy Spirit's abundance, that draws others to you for your provision for both sides of eternity. Thank you I can and do bring these prayers before you in the name of Jesus. Amen.

Think on this: Unless believers are filled to overflowing with the Holy Spirt, there will be no overflow. Do you agree with that? Why or why not? What is God's purpose for that overflowing work of the Spirit? Are there people in your life who need to see and be affected by such an overflow? If so, how is that going to happen and keep on happening?

DAY 100

A Continuing Story

"It seems to me," Stan said, "that each of us who has come to faith should have a story to tell."

"What kind of story?" I asked.

"About what God has done and is doing in our lives," Stan said. "And I think it's supposed to be a long story."

"A long story? Why do you say that?"

"Well," Stan explained, "I'm thinking of what happened when the apostle Paul and his companions returned to Antioch."

"What happened?"

"They told the church in Antioch what had been going on while they were traveling around preaching the gospel. And they had a long story to tell. I think it's supposed to be the same with me and you."

"In what way?" I asked.

"The Book of Acts," Stan replied, "records that Paul and his companions told the disciples in Antioch all that God had done with them. They spent a long time with those disciples. To me, that means the story of all God had done was a long one."

"And you think it should be the same with you?" I asked.

"Sure do," Stan replied. "If I'm open to being used by God for what He wants to accomplish in and through me, I'll have a story to tell others. And by the grace of God, it will be a long one because He was able to work in and through me in many ways."

"If it's a long story, could it get boring?"

"I don't think so," Stan said, "if it's told the way God intends! And it will be, if I follow His lead and share how He allowed me to be part of what He was doing. It's His story, not mine! I just get to tell it."

"And I'm grateful I am now part of it," I said, "because you were willing to help me on my journey."

"And now you can find someone to help," he said, "perhaps even meeting for breakfast while you wait for the train. There are surely enough stories to tell about the wonderful work of God—no matter how many blueberry pancakes you order!"

Bible verses to consider:
And from there they sailed to Antioch, from which they had been commended to the grace of God for the work that they had accomplished. And when they arrived and gathered the church together, they began to report all things that God had done with them and how He had opened a door of faith to the Gentiles. And they spent a long time with the disciples. Acts of the Apostles 14:26-28.

Prayer: Thank you, Father, that you want me to have a story to tell about what you have done in and through me. Thank you, too, that you want that story to be a long one, because of all you have done. I confess that too often I do not have something to tell, because I choose not to be part of your story. Please help me follow your lead, so that you can use me as you intend. And help me tell my story, so that others may know you more deeply and have their own story to tell about you and all you've done in and through them. Thank you I can and do bring these prayers before you in the name of Jesus. Amen.

Think on this: Do you have a story to tell about what God has done in and through you? If no, why? If so, do you want to tell it? Why or why not? Do you believe that if you tell others your story, it may help them want their own story to tell? How can you benefit from listening to others tell what God has done in and through them? Such storytelling can have a positive impact on others, if done as God leads. Would you like that? If so, do you know how to do it?

AFTERWORD

This book would not have been possible if God had not opened the possibility for me to be a part of what He wanted to accomplish. For His gracious provision I am forever thankful.

On this side of eternity there are a number of people who offered encouragement and support all along the way. First, I thank Kay, truly the wife of my youth in whom I rejoice (*Proverbs 5:18*), for all of her support and encouragement every step of the way. This book has involved a lot of time that took me away from her wonderful presence.

Going back to the beginning of my faith walk, I thank Liz for going out of her way to bring me to the truth. She was and is the epitome of hospitality (*Romans 12:*13). Then there was Pastor Bob who played such an important role in building and continuing my faith walk that had started at Peninsula Bible Church.

More recently and specifically with *Waiting for the train* (www.waiting4thetrain.com*)*, I thank who I call "Jim One" for encouraging me to write more after he heard the very first one. Michele encouraged the creation of the blog. "Jim Two" has read and commented on every single blog posting. Gil saw and encouraged the different approach with Biblical truth. David has been immensely helpful with his suggestions for needed changes.

Then there was Nick, who has since boarded the train, who recognized how printed versions of the blog could be used to encourage others. Those printed versions eventually led to this book.

Sarah has done a Facebook page that presents Stan and the *Waiting for the Train* blog in a different format for a different audience. Rhonda provided an excellent hand with editing. Many people at WestBow Press have been amazingly helpful.

To all I say, "Thank you" for the role you have played in getting this book published. And I thank you, the reader, for taking the time to get this far in the book! My hope and prayer is that you have been and will continue to be helped in your faith walk. See you on the other side!

S. Tory Teller